You Are Church!

The life and times of
Louis J. Putz, C.S.C,
prophet, servant, and visionary.

By Bob Ghelardi

Foreword by Reverend Theodore M. Hesburgh C.S.C

D1605647

GOAL/QPC
IMPROVING THE WAY ORGANIZATIONS RUN

You Are Church!
The Life and Times of Louis J. Putz, C.S.C., Prophet, Servant, and Visionary

Karen A. Costura, *Editor*
Janet MacCausland, *Graphic Designer*

GOAL/QPC

12B Manor Parkway, Salem, NH 03079-2862

800.643.4316 or 603.890.8800

Fax: 603.870.9122

E-mail: service@goalqpc.com

www.goalqpc.com

Printed in the United States of America

First Edition   10 9 8 7 6 5 4 3 2 1

ISBN 10: 1-57681-098-4 Hardcover
ISBN 13: 978-1-57681-098-9 Hardcover

ISBN 10: 1-57681-097-6 Paperback
ISBN 13: 978-1-57681-097-2 Paperback

Ask yourself this question... will you follow the outcry of Father Louis Putz, C.S.C., that is "You Are Church"? This was the guiding principle of our hero who declared for years that the Church must revolve around the laity and that laity must understand and accept their responsibility for their "priesthood."

As his close friend, Father David Burrell, C.S.C. stated, *Father Louis implored us to seize the opportunities in our lives for renewal of the Church and to do it now. There is no time to lose as the current situation in the Church suggests.*

This man of unrelenting action continues to inspire and to guide us in the gift **of self** to our Church.

First Mass 1936 Mühldorf
St. Nicholas Church

Foreword

Having written my doctoral dissertation (1945) on baptism as empowering lay apostles, I found myself in tune with Louis Putz's work from the outset.

Despite its location in northern Indiana, Notre Dame has become a crossroads for people from all over the world, bringing fresh perspectives on our rich Catholic tradition. Some people educated here in its earliest days made a lasting mark across the world, like John Zahm, C.S.C. Hearing of Father Zahm's death (in the year of 1921), a Holy Cross candidate for priesthood came to us from Bavaria as a teenager—stimulated by his aunt—a sister of the Holy Cross. Sent to France to study between the wars, he imbibed there a sense of church which he would bring back to Notre Dame on the very cusp of what was in 1939. Louis Putz, C.S.C. never lost his Bavarian roots or accent, yet became the spearhead of a lay apostolate movement which presaged the sense of church as the people of God that dominated the second Vatican council. He lived a life filled with fresh initiatives, starting with creative work with students at Notre Dame and across North America, later combined with publishing ventures which announced (largely through translations) the transformations of Vatican II for an American public, then responding to the call of his congregation of Holy Cross to implement the council as rector of Moreau Seminary at Notre Dame, after which he brought the message of lay involvement in the kingdom of God to retired folks. An incredible list of accomplishments, his true genius lay in having time to hear others' views, and then enticing them to collaborate in implementing them. He had long embodied the view of Vatican II—that "we are church"—as his mode of action inspired others to answer that call.

This biographical study places the man in his times and in ours, offering his witness to rekindle in us the lasting hope for renewal that is the Spirit's message to the churches. As we experience the Spirit working through him, we can dare to glimpse the wonders that same Spirit can and will work through us.

— *Reverend Theodore* M. *Hesburgh*, C.S.C., *President Emeritus,*
   University of Notre Dame

Acknowledgments

James Cunningham, PhD, Professor, University of Pittsburgh; YCS student of Father Putz's at Notre Dame in the 40s.

John Evans, Maine - On Fides staff under Father Putz and member of CFM

Marguerite Corbaci, South Bend, IN - Librarian

Alberta Ross, Professional Specialist in Radiation Lab at Notre Dame. Member of CFM.

Delores K. Herbstreith - Author, Milwaukee, WI

Bill and Carol Dillon, South Bend, IN - CFM Members and bridge players with Father Putz.

Carl and Margie Matthews, Chicago, IL - CFM

Anne Crownshield - Educator, Minneapolis, MN

Dan and Mary Maher - Program Committee Members, Joliet, Il. - CFM

Brother Thomas O' Shaughessy - Former Director of Catholic Charities, South Bend

Sr. Edith Daley, C.S.C. - Former Director of *The Forever Learning Institute*

Frank Quinlivan, C.S.C., Bangladesh - Seminary student under Father Putz

Sam Stanton, Milwaukee - Assistant to Father Putz in Phoenix, AZ

Beverly Eckles - Former Director of *The Forever Learning Institute*

Bill Berg - Furman University, NC

Committee: Reverend David Burrell C.S.C., Hesburgh Chair of Theology and Philosophy, Emeritus, University of Notre Dame; Joe and Jodie Adler, CFM Notre Dame and long-time friend; Bob and Ellen King; Regina Weissert, CFM, Forever Learning Institute Board and long-time friend.

We especially thank Father David Hogan for helping bring this project to light.

From left to right: Fr. Bill Quinn, Fr. James Smyth, Bob Garvey, Fr. Ted Hesburgh

Contents

About the Author

Working on the biography of Fr. Putz has been a challenge and inspiration. To me, it is amazing how much he was able to contribute. I constantly struggle with deciding where to start and when to let go. It left me wanting to take action and follow his example.

In concluding this book, we have included a few of Father Putz's sermons and homilies. It provides the opportunity for further reading and to possibly think about its implication for today. That was after all Father Putz who dreamed to empower the laity to renew the church and society. As the title says, "You are Church!"

Robert Ghelardi worked as a writer with Louis Putz, the leader of Catholic Action in the U.S., during the last two years of his life. As an experienced financial writer Bob is able to illuminate the economic issues that played an unsuspected role in Catholic Action (and the culture's) destiny. Bob has published two other books and completed a third. The first book was *Economics, Society and Culture*, published to good reviews by Dell and Delta. The second (as coauthor) was *Power and Authority in the Catholic Church* (about Cardinal Cody), published by the University of Notre Dame Press.

As a one-time speech writer for several of America's top executives, Bob Ghelardi knows how to craft messages to target audiences and is confident this book will be a referendum on the state of the Catholic Church today. Bob doesn't believe that he has either a theological "liberal" nor a "conservative" bias. He is a Catholic who believes in a spiritual world that has direct relevance to secular life.

Insights

from a Mentor of Putz: Fr. Jean Daniélou

Real apostolic zeal requires us to love only for Christ's Sake, and never for our own: it means that we may never do anything with the idea of keeping people to ourselves, because it consists in such a great love of souls as to make us happy in their welfare even when it is none of our doing. That is the essence and the specific character of disinterested love: we must be glad whenever any good influence is at work; there must be no monopolizing of a soul. The importance of this rule is capital, for the alternative is self-seeking, a hidden corruption to destroy the purity of apostolic zeal. But this is not by any means to say that a harmful influence should not be vigorously attacked: in this situation, the case is altered, for we have no right to acquiesce in the subjection of a soul which is under our care, or connected with us in any way, to bad influences. If it is our duty to be unselfishly glad of every good influence, it is just as much our duty to fight to save souls from what we know is bad for them. Christ's spouse must not turn adulteress: we sought to have that intuitive quickness of perception, that penetrating insight which will enable us to detect, almost to feel, an infidelity. For we know that the seducer is none other than Satan, who was once an angle of light, and who can use the outward appearance of goodness for his purpose of enticing a soul away from whatever is really good for it. Sometimes he will turn a soul back from the true course of its own perfection by the attraction of something else that is good in itself, but less perfect, and represents for that particular soul a real infidelity. We must be able to defend souls against themselves: it is all part of apostolic zeal.

Such zeal springs originally from the love of God, but it comes from the love of men too; for we know that the real happiness and full perfection of men consists in fidelity to their calling and to the love of God. We have to help others to be true to themselves, help them to serve in their own main task and to obey God's call to each one of them. So doing, we shall further at one and the same time both the rightful claims to God upon each soul, and the best interests of the souls of men. If this is our aim, with a purely spiritual and holy motive, and also with some degree of supernatural intensity of purpose (for the love of God is a devouring fire) then we have spiritual zeal, which is apostolic and godly.

Cardinal Jean Daniélou

Cardinal Jean Deniélou († 1974) was a French Jesuit, a theologian, and a peritus at Vatican II

Louis Putz Family when Louis was age 12

"Father Putz understands precisely and fully what the lay
apostolate is; he knows what it has done; he has a vision of what it can do.
Not the least merit of his book is its practical and realistic approach to the
problems necessarily involved in making the lay apostolate effective.
He has no illusions about the difficulty; he has no grandiose schemes
to propose and no easy solutions to offer."

The Modern Apostle by Louis J. Putz, CSC (1957) Foreword by Bishop Leo. A. Pursley

"The Altar bread is ground out of many individual grains
into one bread and the wine is pressed out of many grapes into one drink.
This is the image of the People of God at Mass. All the varied and diversified
elements at Mass, representing a cross section of the world...all of them are
needed so that Christ can grow into maturity as a Mystical Body."

The Modern Apostle by Louis J. Putz, CSC (1957) p. 29

Chapter 1

A Dream Comes True

Ludwig (Louis) Josef Putz Jr. was born on June 1, 1909. He was the first of three children of Ludwig Sr. Putz and Anna Leidman Putz, then living in a log farmhouse in Simbach, a village in eastern Bavaria across a river from Hitler's Austrian birthplace.

Putz's father was a railroad engineer, and his occupation saved him from service in the army during World War I. His son remembered him as strong, demanding and domineering, the opposite of himself, and as mostly absent.

Shortly after Louis was born, the family moved to nearby Erding. Louis' mother nursed him through a severe bout of pneumonia when he was four while still caring for the second child, Frances. The last child was delivered into the world by a midwife in a family bedroom. Enrolling Louis in the local elementary school, Anna impressed upon him the supreme importance of education, and to please her he strove to do well. He attended mass twice each week to pray for the German army.

Louis especially enjoyed the religion classes taught at the school by parish priests. He spent evenings in a day-care center run by a nun who fostered in him a vocation to become a priest himself. At the age of seven, he confided to her that was what he intended to do, and she advised him to receive Communion and pray about it every Sunday for nine weeks.

After almost three years of war, a rumor flew through the village that the Americans were coming from "across the water" to join the enemy. The only water Louis had ever seen was Sempe Creek behind his family home, so he began watching it closely for American troops who would wade across it and make trouble for the Putz family. Soon, he had a vivid dream—powerful and mysterious. In the dream, the Americans appeared on the far side of the stream, but instead of crossing, they beckoned to him to come to them. What could this mean? Weren't they the enemy? The dream haunted him for the next several years.

Louis spent his summers during the war on the farm of his maternal grandmother, also named Anna, a woman as kind and generous as her daughter, and a born educator who sped along his development. With her daughter Elizabeth, youngest of nine children, she raised wheat, oats, barley, apples, pears, and cherries, and kept two milk cows, pigs, and a flock of chickens. Louis was the third hand and earned his keep by gathering fresh apples and pears that had fallen from the fruit trees during the night for the pigs. He collected wood for the stove and hauled water from the outside pumps. Anna led the family in the rosary every night and insisted that one of them attend Mass each day. Frequently it was Louis, and he would then eat breakfast at the rectory, where his aunts Katherine and Maria worked. Postcards poured in from relatives on the French, Belgian, Russian and Italian fronts. Uncles returned on leaves to do the heavy work—slaughtering, plowing, harvesting —police spied on the family to prevent violation of the meat-rationing laws. In a document he wrote at the end of his life, Putz recalled his father standing in the door of their home with a rifle, ready to repel the Bolsheviks who briefly took over Munich and Bavaria (an incident that caused great difficulty for the papal nuncio, Eugenio Pacelli, later Pope Pius XII).

My First Communion, 1920.

In 1920, Putz's parents moved again, to Muehldorf, where Louis was enrolled in a progressive school that taught mathematics, the sciences and modern languages rather than the classical curriculum of the traditional gymnasiums. In 1922, his aunt, a member of the Sisters of the Holy Cross who was working at St. Mary's College in Notre Dame, Indiana, arrived in Simbach for the celebration of the golden wedding anniversary of her parents, and Ludwig Sr.'s parents, an event that Louis recalled as the high point of his childhood. She overheard an argument between the father and his son. As a youth, Ludwig Sr. had aspired to join the Capuchin order but was turned away. When his son was young, the father registered him for entrance at the Capuchin Seminary in Burghausen, Bavaria. Now Louis was telling his father that he indeed wanted to become a priest but not a Capuchin, because Capuchins wore beards. The aunt chirped that he should go to America. Not a bad idea, in fact. Germany was undergoing economic difficulty at the time, and America was the "Promised Land." But the idea seemed far-fetched.

Almost a year later, in May 1923, a letter arrived from the aunt telling Louis that she had enrolled him at Holy Cross Seminary at the University of Notre Dame in South Bend, Indiana, and that a ticket for a trans-Atlantic crossing would follow shortly. Louis was 14 years old. Now the meaning of the dream that haunted him seemed to become clear. He would go, even though separation would be traumatic for him and his mother. This was the first self-defining decision of his life, and it remained the farthest-reaching. His father reluctantly agreed to escort him to Hamburg for the August 4th, 1922, departure, but pleaded with him the whole way there to reconsider.

The aunt had secured the money from the bishop of Fresno, California, her close friend for whom she went to work that summer. It was a generous bishop who would fund a prospect for someone else's seminary. A few days after the ship weighed anchor, the U.S. Congress curtailed immigration so sharply that Louis would have been excluded had he waited.

A Lutheran family on the ship—the Sternals—relatives of the cook in the St. Mary's convent, were also going to South Bend, and Louis was placed with them. He and the family remained friends for the rest of his life, and three of the daughters became Catholics. Louis impressed the family by reading the entire New Testament during the trip; he said later that he had only read the text because there had been nothing else to read. When the ship docked in New York on August 15, Louis was shocked to see hundreds laboring on the piers and terminals. A new world, indeed!

Another shock: at Ellis Island, he was separated from the Sternal family and detained because the Holy Cross priest instructed to meet him failed to show up. When a huge and surly German-speaking immigration officer asked Putz, implying strong disapproval, if he wanted to become a priest as his papers indicated, the boy defensively stated, "No, I want to get to America to pick up the loose dollars lying on every street." So his aunt in California and a superior at Notre Dame were contacted and asked for sworn statements that they would care for the boy if he failed to become a priest. Nine days slowly passed. For all Louis knew, he would remain forever on Ellis Island, where pandemonium ruled over a vast array of tongues and a swarm of oddly different struggling groups. Louis witnessed several knife fights, took solace from a kindly African woman and huddled with the German contingent. The food was new and strange: hot cereal, sweet potatoes, scrambled eggs and ham, and French toast with syrup. The Germans relied on Louis's rapport with a police officer to help them regain the same beds every night, avoiding bedbugs, fleas and contagions. When the affidavits for Louis arrived, the immigration officer casually asked Louis if he still did not want to be a priest. Louis said, "No, I do." The officer astonishingly replied, "Why didn't you say so? You'd be in South Bend by now!"

On August 24th, Louis was given $25 and put on a Grand Trunk train looping through Canada toward South Bend. A note was pinned to his shirt: "Deliver me to South Bend, Indiana." Not knowing how to count the money, he starved for most of the trip, although a Swede gave him a sandwich and he bought himself another in Paris, Ontario. He arrived in South Bend exhausted and hungry, at 2 a.m. on August 25th, the feast day of St. Louis. The trainmaster summoned the police and requested a German-speaking officer, eliciting a cop named Shricker, a member of the Ku Klux Klan, who took Louis in his sidecar for cake and coffee at the home of his parents. After a snack, Louis went off again in the sidecar to Walsh Hall on the Notre Dame campus, where at 4 a.m., a Brother Amadeus put him to bed, only to awaken him an hour later for Mass in the crypt chapel beneath the Sacred Heart church. There, to Louis's bewilderment, several Masses were in progress, none with any attendants. Taken to breakfast in the Main Building, he met a few seniors in Holy Cross Seminary, two of whom spoke German. Since his meager baggage and his violin were still in New York, a German-speaking priest later took him to town to buy him a suit.

The rector of Holy Cross, Fr. Finnegan, was friendly and Louis began to feel comfortable. German sisters working in the kitchen and the laundry became fond of him and protective. For the rest of his life, Louis would form close attachments with women such as he had with his mother. The sisters took him around to meet Germans in South Bend.

Louis received yet another shock. Underclassmen were forbidden to associate with seniors, and when the juniors arrived just after Labor Day, that rule went into effect and prevented Louis from talking to his only friends, the seniors. The spiritual director of the junior class, Fr. McElhone, told Louis to model himself on another priest, Fr. Margraf, who also had come from Germany as a young boy but who, much unlike Louis, was highly athletic. Fr. McElhone favored vigorous sports such as football, basketball and hockey, and perhaps feared that Louis's partiality to chess, cards and reading signaled homosexuality, a temptation which the prohibition on contact between the juniors and seniors was meant to forestall. However, no one gave any concrete reasons for this to Louis.

Louis's best friend was Fr. Finnegan, the superior, who applauded his excellent grades. Putz later said that Fr. Finnegan saved his sanity by putting him the first summer with an American farm family in Granger with ten children, the Carricos, with whom he could share the farm work he loved. The warm family relieved the intense loneliness Louis had known during his first months in South Bend. He also worked on a farm operated by the Holy Cross Brothers at Rolling Prairie, where he picked fruit for the market and cared for Bill Rockne, the mentally retarded son of Knute Rockne. As physically gifted as his father, Bill sometimes beat Louis up, but Louis did not report the beatings because he feared he would be blamed. A retired Superior General, Fr. Francais, who Putz said spoke less English than he did, was living there, and was delighted to speak French with Louis. During this first summer, Louis became a sort of ward of seminarian Howard Kenna, who later would play a pivotal role in Louis's life. He also met four boys who remained thereafter among his dearest friends: Lawrence Graner, later archbishop of Dacca (in the future Pakistan); Phil Moore, future director of graduate studies at Notre Dame; Henry Bolger (Professor and chairman of the University of Notre Dame physics department, 1936–1964); and a boy named Daugherty, whom Putz would succeed briefly as chaplain at the Marianite Provincialate in Princeton, New Jersey. But for the next eight years, Putz did not leave the Notre Dame campus for as much as a day, except to attend a community camp with the other seminarians.

After two years, Finnegan was named bishop of Helena, Montana, and was replaced at Holy Cross by a Fr. Earley, a martinet whom Louis thought preferred his dog to people. Earley singled out Louis for menial labor during the lonely and hot summers, appointing him to be janitor, dishwasher, maid and messenger, all without a word of recognition. Earley also appropriated Louis's only spending money, the tips he earned as a waiter for guests. His violin, which had arrived from New York, lay unused, because music lessons were forbidden, and it soon vanished. The priest objected to Louis's collection of valuable European stamps as an unnecessary distraction, and his Roman missal was also banished because the boys prayed the rosary at Mass. Louis's only friends in this penal regime were the German laundry nuns, until he formed close and enduring attachments to fellow seminarians George Schidel and Joseph Barry.

The schoolwork was rigorous in nature. Louis earned high grades in Latin, Greek and French, but his lessons in German were discontinued and he received no direction in English studies, nor any math or science. A Latin teacher, Fr. Miller, took strong exception to Louis' upstart notion that the English language had been influenced as heavily by German and French as by Latin. The classes were uniform for all students, with no consultation or variation for talents and background. Putz became the class brain, but was frustrated by his proximity to vistas behind doors locked to seminarians.

Putz began his formal novitiate in August, 1927, under Fr. Donahue, a former Superior General and a follower of St. Bernard and a believer in physical correction. Putz loathed these ideals. Louis suffered greatly from a lack of personal closeness with any human being. He later wrote that on January 6th, he had a mystical experience that remained with him for the remainder of his life. He thought that God touched him and demonstrated that even if his superiors and confreres were not interested in him, God was. His chosen spiritual director transmitted to Louis his own devotion to St. Theresa, the "Little Flower." Years later, when studying in France, Louis made pilgrimages to the saint's shrine in Lisieux and attended Cardinal Pacelli's dedication of her basilica.

The bland uniformity continued after Louis entered college at Notre Dame, except that visits to the library were permitted and some of the Notre Dame faculty took a personal interest in talented students and gave them advice, even though association with faculty members, whether secular or clerical (even the great scientist Fr. Nieuwland), was strongly discouraged. Few outside contacts were allowed, and the seminarians were encouraged to gather in groups rather than in pairs or, worse, going alone. The training in philosophy, Louis later recalled as being superficial and dictated by Rome. He graduated magna cum laude with praise for his accomplishments in English and German. His classmate, Frank O'Malley, later famous at Notre Dame, graduated summa cum laude, a portent of things to come. What Louis remembered best about his four years of college was the tedium; he called them the least productive years of his life.

Putz visits with his Aunt, Sr. Marroma C.S.C., who encouraged him to come to Notre Dame.

After his graduation, a Holy Cross priest named Raymond Murray offered to have Louis Putz admitted to Harvard University. However, when Fr. Steiner, the provincial superior, was approached with this notion, he roared, "We're not spending any money on you!" His next assignment routinely would have been for theology at Holy Cross College in Washington, D.C., but he had taken the "fourth vow" to serve in the missions, and that summer the General Chapter of the Congregation of Holy Cross met at Moreau Seminary on the Notre Dame campus and decided that a missioner could be assigned anywhere in the world. It also slated for rehabilitation the congregation's natal province in France, which had fallen into decline, and it decided that Putz and another student, John Biger, should go there for theology. Putz was singled out partly because when four French seminarians had stopped at Moreau on their way from Canada to France, he was able to speak with them in French. It occurred to Louis that it might be inconvenient to be a German citizen living in France in 1932, so he asked for a delay because he was on schedule to become a United States citizen in December. The order's Superior General assured him no war between France and Germany was in the cards, and told him to go. That decision almost cost Putz his life, and also changed it fatefully. So, off went Putz and Biger, along with Fr. Pinson, the French provincial and a brother named Ernest to Le Mans, France. On the boat, another passenger, Cardinal Verdier of Paris, confided to them his plans to build 100 churches around Paris to serve the huge influx of people coming into the suburbs.

While awaiting the completion of a residence for them, the new seminarians were lodged in the diocesan seminary at Le Mans, an advantage because they learned the customs and jargon of the French clergy and mingled freely with the local people. In the second year, the seminarians moved into a Holy Cross house while continuing to take their theology at the Grand Seminaire. Putz befriended the rector, Fr. Leroux, and especially Fr. Jules Lebreton, a teacher of moral theology and chaplain to a movement called the "Young Christian Workers" or, in its French acronym, JOC. Because Putz was the only typist in the building, Fr. Lebreton conscripted him as a secretary and asked him to type up notes that discussed the JOC movement. Putz also saw local students coming to visit Lebreton on Saturdays, and he became curious about the movement. Lebreton explained it to Louis and introduced him to a Msgr. Guerin, the movement's national chaplain. Thus, Putz encountered one of two important developments in the Church in Europe (or the world) in that century. Its generic name was Catholic Action. He was soon to encounter a second important development.

The building into which the seminarians moved in 1933 was the old church built by the Holy Cross order's founder, Fr. Basil Moreau, as the chapel to the College de Sainte Croix. Central to the order's renewal in France was a rehabilitation of the sites where Moreau had labored, and especially important were this chapel (that had afterwards become a barracks and then a horse barn) and the house where he died. Putz was charged with the chapel's long-neglected garden and landscaping. He also ran the wine cellars, ordering many barrels of wine each year, half of which were bottled, the other half served at table. The superior, the half-deaf Fr. Vanier, relied on Louis heavily. Vanier's pet project was to collect and archive all papers and materials connected with the life of Fr. Moreau, so Louis scavenged through the chancery for manuscripts and documents, and through the files of local newspapers to save disintegrating editions published during the Founder's life. The seminarians' only link with the United States and Notre Dame now was the English newspapers they picked up on Monday mornings that gave the Notre Dame football scores, including that of the famous 1935 victory against Ohio State. Putz believed he would remain in France for the rest of his life.

For his final year of theology, Putz went to the Catholic Institute of Theology in Paris, where among his professors were the heralds of a new theology—Frs. Yves Congar, Henri De Lubac and Jean Danielou, who after the war, and along with the famous Cardinal Suhard, would meet regularly for discussions with the papal nuncio to France, Angelo Roncalli (who would later be named Pope John XXIII). Even as he was introduced to the new JOC lay movement, Putz was sitting at the feet of the masters of a new theology of the laity for a Church it described as "the people of God." He also met Teilhard de Chardin, a Jesuit professor at the Institute, and a dogma professor named Fr. Dion, later chaplain to the French Underground and the last man the Nazis executed before they evacuated Paris after the Normandy invasion.

In his book *The Modern Apostle*, Putz shares some of the influences of Monsignor Cardijn on his thinking:

"Monsignor Cardijn happened upon a very normal and natural formula, and almost by accident. From his seminary days he had decided to dedicate all his life to the cause of the young workingman. He himself came from a worker's family. His father was the victim of over-work in order to be able to educate his son for the priesthood. But young Father Joseph Cardijn soon noticed that his grade school youngsters quickly lost interest in religion after they left his catechism class. He wanted to find out what happened to the youngsters who entered the ranks of the workers.

He got a group of them to promise to return week after week to report back to him the daily experiences and happenings in their worker environment. Then he helped them to form a Christian conscience about the daily struggle and even challenged them to offset some of the handicaps by individual and group initiatives. The famous formula of "observe, judge, act" was born and St. Thomas Aquinas had already figured it out as the normal method of human prudence. Every prudent action must be based on good observation or consultation, on a judgment as to ways and means, and finally on a decision to engage in action."

When Putz encountered Congar and De Lubac, the Depression was propelling the Nazis to power in Germany and the Left to power in France, where Labor and Communist parties battled the Right in the streets. As the Church tried to cope with Fascist and Communist regimes throughout Europe, the Catholic Actionists in the name of the old faith challenged the secular youth movements on both sides. When Hitler seized the Rhineland, tensions in Paris became almost unbearable.

The Holy Cross order staffed three parishes in Paris suburbs where Cardinal Verdier had built churches. The pastor at Ormesson, Fr. Celeste Niard, asked Putz to assist him with new JOC cells. Therefore, each weekend Putz went to Ormesson, in the "Red" (Communist) District, where he worked closely with four youth cells, each associated with a distinct occupation: high school, university, agriculture, and sailors and shipbuilders. They battled the communists, who were multiplying after France's traditional foe, Germany, turned fascist. Leon Bloy struggled to maintain his "communard" government in Paris.

Putz with Diaconate class, 1935

After Louis finished his theology courses (and received a theology degree magna cum laude), Fr. Baudet, the rector in Le Mans, announced that Louis had won the prize as the best theology student. The bishop who was to give the award had already bestowed on Putz the subdiaconate and diaconate, but when he belatedly learned that Putz was German, he instead gave the new prize to an Alsatian, greatly embarrassing Putz, the seminary and the rector. Putz resolved that he would not accept ordination from that bishop and, returned to Paris to be ordained with a class of strangers who, after the ceremony, decamped to celebrate with their families while Putz sat alone in the church.

A nurse approached and begged him to go with her to a hospital, where the mother of the hospital's chief executive lay dying. Anti-clerical French law forbade a priest to enter a hospital except at a patient's explicit and personal request, but the mother, still lucid, feared her son would be fired if it became known that she had summoned a priest. So Putz was smuggled in, gave the woman the final rites behind a hastily erected screen, and discreetly departed. This prophetically ended Louis Putz's first day as a priest: alone with a small clutch of lay persons in extremis. Within a few days he celebrated his first Mass, no family in attendance, at the church in Ormesson, as the Communist youth marched and howled outside. The date was April 11, 1936. A group stood in the door chanting the Internationale as Putz intoned the prayers. He was thrilled. He was at the heart of the Church's struggle and his priestly career had only begun.

What had led Louis Putz to this moment were two creative movements in the Catholic Church in the 20th Century: the New Theology movement and Catholic Action movement.

Before first mass, 1936

"It is difficult to love God with one's whole soul, heart, mind
and strength and not do it in the state of life and environment where
God has placed us."

The Modern Apostle by Louis J. Putz, CSC (1957) p. 62

Chapter 2

Louis Putz's Unique Formation as a Priest

Shortly after Louis Putz's ordination, his superior, Fr. Pinson, put him in charge of a minor seminary at Dinan on the Breton coast where Pinson lived and where Putz enjoyed a summer among the Breton fishermen. In contrast to the Germanic Putz, Pinson was highly mercurial and would change his mind three or four times a day even on important matters. One evening he asked Fr. Putz to lead the morning meditation, awoke him at 3 a.m. to announce that he would do it himself, and then threw the responsibility back into Putz's lap at 6 a.m. Pinson became a thorn in Putz's side.

Pinson cherished his reputation as a wine connoisseur, and one day invited all the regional superiors to a dinner at the seminary to celebrate his birthday. During the repast he gave Putz the key to the third wine cellar, reserved for the finest wines, and requested a bottle of the best vintage. When Putz brought it and poured a sample, Pinson remonstrated: "Non, non, non! Bring me another bottle." But the second bottle brought a similar response: "Non! Bring me a third." Instead, Putz retrieved the first bottle from a table behind Pinson, pretended to open it, and poured a sample as the guests watched. "C'est ca, that is the best wine!" Fr. Pinson exclaimed. To his bewilderment the table erupted in laughter.

The next day Pinson summoned Louis into the seminary garden. He paced, pulled his beard and blurted out: "Fr. Putz, you are a pillar of the community, and they need you again in Le Mans."

So Louis Putz was put in charge of the seminarians at Le Mans, his beloved earlier home for three years. He began to help to organize JOC at the local parish, Notre Dame de Sainte Croix, and soon was in charge of all the Catholic Action in the diocese. Among other activities, he conducted retreats and celebrated Masses in the woods and in chapels. He would face the altar toward the people and say the Mass in French, practices not countenanced by the rules. Here, in his earliest priesthood, he was using the liturgy as a way to form the lay apostolate while nurturing and expressing community—what the coming liturgical movement would specify as the liturgy's essential purposes. He saw Eucharist and liturgy as intimately united with service, as at their common founding at the "Last Supper," when Christ washed the apostles' feet. Later he noted the dramatic contrast between this experience and what he had witnessed at his first (simultaneous) Masses at Notre Dame, when half a dozen priests were saying separate Masses alone.

The whole Church, triumphant, suffering, and militant, participates in the unique priesthood of Christ and in His victim hood. Humanity united to Christ at Mass becomes the priest and the victim. The Mass is therefore not an individualistic act of piety. It is a family or social act. All mankind is interested, all mankind needs to be associated. Through it, man as an individual and mankind as a unit is reunited to God. This union effected through the Holy Sacrifice is the source of an all-embracing spirituality.

Father Louis J. Putz, C.S.C.

Putz's early formation as a priest was unlike that of any other priest who had ever worked in the United States. This is crucial to his significance. Catholic Action demanded constant interaction among lay people aiming at common solutions for practical problems based on Christian principles. It was communal in that its smallest unit was a group. Equally significant is that the correct and best solution 1) was unknown at the start of the inquiry, and 2) not only could be discovered only through the interaction inside the group and between it and its environment, but also was usually a surprise, unexpected and unpredictable. No individualistic development or discernment could spark such a process, nor could any bureaucracy. The cell's members knew that everything depended on them, not individually, but in their common action. They had to examine the situation together with their own minds, probe it so as to distinguish its components and generate a change or solution which the group would try to execute. They were told that only so they could grow as persons and as Christians. Their social prosperity and their personal and spiritual development were tied to this process. This was and is quite different from the Catholic bureaucracy, where direction mainly comes from above. "Specialized" Catholic Action was something new in the Catholic Church since the Middle Ages, and a reversal of the Church's method of organizing since that time. The bureaucracy assumed it had the basic answers for everything, but it had the answers for nothing, for its principles were useless without this other dimension. Specialized Catholic Action restarted the culture- and community-building process long dormant in the Catholic Church. And in CA's intense give-and-take of inter-personal engagement in spiritual and social life, Louis Putz was permanently formed as a priest. Once he had seen and experienced its truth, nothing could convince him that he had not seen it or that it wasn't true. Among American priests, he was one of the few who had really seen it. The most ardent other champions of the new movement were the popes, at least six of them, while its strongest foes were among the bishops, who thought Catholic Action smacked too much of the Communism it tried to fight.

Putz soon learned another lesson he never forgot. When consulted, his bishop, while refusing to give permission for Putz's unorthodox practices (Putz later praised him for honesty), also declined to intervene, saying that Fr. Putz, as head of the youth groups, had to make the liturgies attractive to them. Putz learned, and remembered, that it's easier to ask for forgiveness than permission; "If you ask permission, they almost have to say no." In 1937, Putz attended the national JOC congress at a large Paris stadium, where the elaborate ceremonies made an impression on him that remained for the rest of his life.

During his residency in France, Louis Putz began a deep devotion to two saints who were exemplary doers. One was Vincent de Paul, of whom Putz read a famous multi-volume biography in French. He thereafter explored the Parisian scenes of the great man's life. The other, St. Paul, became the second model for Putz's life, for Paul was the missionary to the Gentiles, built the first church communities, and clashed with his own Jewish community of Pharisees and many small-minded Christians. Paul endured great hardships in moving from place to place, while making great disciples. Putz, in his Catholic Action work, came to resemble Paul in all these ways.

In light of his activity in JOC, and as he contrasted his experience as student and director in the French seminary system with that in the seminaries he had endured in the United States, Putz began to see the need for a reform of curricula and practices. Seminary formation should revolve around responsibility, he concluded—the exact opposite of his training at the tranquil Holy Cross Seminary in South Bend. Then, on September 1, 1939, Hitler invaded Poland, triggering World War II and stranding the German citizen Putz in France. He received a telegram from his order's new superior general ordering him back to Notre Dame at once but not suggesting how to do it.

Now began a drama that further separated Putz from other priests while confirming his faith in Catholic Action's vision. It produced incidents that a faith-minded person could take to be miracles, and in interpreting them so, Putz sealed in his soul Catholic Action's view of the individual's relationship with God. The experience played the role in his life that Mao's Long March did for the Chinese Communists and it made him skeptical of the charismatic movement that flourished in the American Church during the 1970s. This was the first time Putz felt called upon to act out Catholic Action principles as a lone individual.

The day after the order from his superior, Putz hurried to the U.S. Embassy, open on Saturday only, because of the crisis. He was assigned to the Vice Consul, Weissburger, who refused to accept the superior's telegram as proof that the German-speaking Putz was a U.S. citizen. No explanations availed. Putz could have sent himself the telegram, Weissburger said. At last the consul had an idea: he asked Putz what shirt factory was in South Bend. Putz replied at once: "The Wilson factory." He then pulled down his collar to show Weissburger the Wilson label on his own shirt. The vice-consul, a relative of the shirt-making Wilson family, was convinced and stamped a U.S. visa on Putz's swastika-festooned German passport.

But when Putz walked out of the embassy the French police seized him and, without a trial or processing, put him into an internment camp improvised in a suburban soccer stadium, where he was held for three months. Foreseeing a long imprisonment, or death, whether or not the Nazis arrived (his father had been dismissed from his railroad job for objecting to the Nazi regime), Putz sought out the camp's commander to volunteer as a chaplain. This official turned out to be a World War I general who had become a priest. He declared that he had enough priests in his ranks and wanted no more in his camp. So he allowed Putz to amble over to a nearby church ostensibly to obtain the vestments and instruments needed for saying Masses and hearing confessions, and then turned a blind eye as Putz ambled on down the road and back to Le Mans. If Putz had not escaped that camp, he probably was a dead man.

The next day, Sunday, as he intoned a Spanish version of Tantum Ergo during the ceremony of Benediction in Le Mans, Putz realized with panic that the cadences eerily recalled those of Deutschland, Deutschland Uber Alles, a popular German patriotic song. He was sure the congregation would rise up. Should he stop, explain, or run? The hymn dragged on interminably, but the parishioners still noticed nothing. The next day Putz surrendered to the civilian authorities, claiming that the parish needed him, that he hated Hitler, loved France and wanted to remain there. Surprisingly, the atheist prefect agreed, stipulating only that the bishop assume responsibility for Putz's conduct and safety. However, the bishop refused. The charitable interpretation is that he knew he could not ensure Putz's safety.

Now Putz realized that he must—at all hazards and however improbably—find and reach a ship. He first solicited from a parish member, a former general of the French Fourth Division in World War I, a letter of introduction and passage. Next, he sought out a seminarian who had worked for the French line, and this youth tapped his contacts to learn that a French ship would depart on November 11 from Le Havre, a French port under British control. On November 9, Putz caught a train to Paris, and there sought refuge in a local convent. That night an air-raid alarm sent him and the nuns scurrying to the cellar, where they noticed his accent and began to look at him suspiciously. Therefore, he cleared out and found a train bound for Le Havre. There the French line clerks would neither sell him a ticket nor reveal whether a ship was sailing at all. The line was not acknowledging departures for fear that the Nazi U-boats would be the first to know. The clerks insisted there was no ship. Distraught, Putz retreated to the men's room. As he entered, a girl standing nearby spotted his JOC button and followed him in. She whispered the number of the pier the French ship would be sailing from and urged him immediately to take a taxi there, ticket or no ticket. The taxi was detained by British marines who demanded his papers. Hiding his swastika-emblazoned passport, Putz produced the letter from the French general. The marines could not read the French but recognized the official markings. Putz then announced that he was on an urgent special mission. The soldiers escorted him to the ship, whisked him past the French Line ticket takers and put him in First Class. He locked the door until the ship was well into the English Channel. Somehow his papers passed inspection at Southampton, the clerks probably assuming that since he was on the ship he was legitimate. Putz then bought a tourist ticket for the remainder of the journey to New York. However, after noticing his command of three languages, the captain put Putz back into First Class, where he enjoyed good food while translating for others. The passengers were petrified by reports that the great German battleship Bismarck, having just sunk two British cruisers, was patrolling the area for new prey. Fortunately, the Bismarck knew not only that Putz's ship was there (the French precautions were futile) but also that it was carrying only civilians. The Bismarck decided to wait for the ship's return passage.

When the ship arrived in New York on the 21st of November, the French officers listed Putz last on the manifest, probably expecting trouble. But the immigration officers scanned the list and called him out first as the French officers sputtered and fretted. One customs official frowned sternly at Putz and asked, "How come Notre Dame lost to Iowa?" The main officer was an Iowa graduate, his assistant from Notre Dame. The latter with some deft questions verified Putz's origin. Putz wanted to kiss the floor. The relieved French officers broke into smiles and a party broke out. Putz, however, hurried to the New York Central office to buy a ticket to South Bend, but he discovered that he didn't have enough money. The agent directed him to the seventh floor to request a half-price clergy ticket. There an attendant sought to verify Putz's clerical status by looking him up in the Catholic Directory. With a sinking heart Putz realized that he was not listed in it because he was ordained in France. The attendant searched for the name that Putz knew was not there. Nevertheless, there it was; Louis Putz, pastor of Blessed Sacrament church, Waterloo, Iowa. "Yeah, you're good," said the assistant, handing Putz the ticket book. (Author's note: Putz would later visit his namesake to thank him and to share a good laugh.) But as he sped sadly over the sleeping prairies ever farther from France, Putz grieved that his career in Catholic Action was over.

The story is amusing, but for Putz the issue was life or death. He escaped partly because he started during the "phony war" before the front erupted. Nevertheless, the JOC-ist principles for self-starting action that guided him made the difference. How many other priests could or would have acted so? It is unlikely that many would have done so. They would have invoked their clerical privileges and the grace of God— perhaps successfully, too. What Putz confirmed for himself was that God will activate Himself if we will do the same. That is how he preferred to work.

Young Christian Workers (YCW) – Young Christian Students (YCS) Group, 1945

Father Putz in Paris

"(Speaking of Young Christian Workers) A person does not save himself merely by acts of religion. Going to Mass and the sacraments does not mean much if we are not motivated by charity. And it's precisely by loving God with our whole mind, heart, soul and strength and one's neighbor, too, that we fulfill the law of God. Obviously that can be done only in the day-in, day-out, run-of-the-mill sort of life. I think we have to be convinced that salvation is a matter of living one's life totally, integrally."

The Modern Apostle by Louis J. Putz, C.S.C. (1957) p. 81

Paris, 1936, just before ordination

Chapter 3

The Growth of Young Christian Students (YCS)

The targets of Notre Dame's Catholic Action had been almost everything but students, but at the end of the war, Catholic Action turned its attention to the student body. In November of 1945, the British National Union of Students hosted student "leaders" from almost 40 nations in an effort to revive the pre-war international student movement. The precise value of such an organization is difficult to gauge from a distance of almost 60 years. In Europe, students were the group least crushed by the war's destruction, and they were politically active. The London conference brought to birth the International Union of Students (IUS), complete with a charter and a constitution. The first meeting of this IUS was scheduled for August 1946, in Prague, Czechoslovakia. Why that city was the choice is not clear, but it favored the machinations of Communist elements who wanted to capture the IUS for the Kremlin, as they had many other front organizations, such as the World Federation of Trade Unions.

Fr. John Courtney Murray became alarmed and presented in the April 13, 1946, issue of the Jesuit journal *America* an analysis and a proposal for a response. He wanted to see "Catholic youth...put on the move in the international field, in a solidly organized movement, with a truly conquering spirit, that will continue through a positive program and also combat Communistic influence." He said that a group of students should be selected, intensely trained by subject matter experts and sent to the Prague meeting. It may not have occurred to Murray that such a group working at the behest of shadowy organizers would not have been in students' own best interests.

The international preparatory committee of the IUS assigned 25 delegate seats to each of the superpowers, and lesser numbers to smaller countries on a sliding scale. The committee's American members decided that students from Catholic and Protestant universities would receive four seats each and that the remaining 17 seats would be filled "democratically." Murray intended to select the Catholic delegates from Jesuit colleges in the northeast, but a Notre Dame student by the name of Vince Hogan persuaded him in a letter to include the colleges of other orders and regions. Murray invited Hogan and his colleague Martin McLaughlin to join 11 other Catholic students at Ridgeley Manor, the country estate of Mrs. Frances E. Leggett in New York's Catskill Mountains. There, for three weeks they studied the Prague conference's agenda, specified and prioritized goals, planned strategies and assigned responsibilities to each of the seven students who ultimately went to Europe. Three of these seven were women who attended a series of meetings of Catholic students throughout Europe. The other four, Hogan, McLaughlin, Henry Briefs of Georgetown, and Edward Kirchner, a member of the international Catholic student organization, Pax Romana, would go to Prague.

When Murray became ill and could not accompany them, McLaughlin suggested Putz as the ideal replacement: multilingual, with a rich European background, close ties to the French JEC, highly experienced with student apostolates, and deeply involved in Catholic Action. At least, that is the official story. McLaughlin says the reason Murray decided on Putz as a replacement was because he was 6'4" tall and bald, and would stand out in the crowd. It strains credulity, but who knows? Murray called Putz, who hurried to New York in June 1946, to join the delegation. On the ship, it became clear that the American delegation was diverse and fractious. The Catholics and Protestants were suspicious of each other, while the remainder ranged from highly conservative to Communist. Even functional unity, let alone consensus, would be elusive.

In Europe, the Catholic contingent left the larger group to make brief stops in England and France. In Liverpool, they inspected a successful Young Christian Workers (YCW) group. In France, they attended a JEC congress that was attempting to return JEC to its pre-war strength. Putz was horrified by the devastation he saw on the continent and was shocked to discover that even his own father and stepmother had perished under American bombs in the last weeks of the war. He went to Bavaria to console his family, of whom he had not seen since well before the war. Putz also met with a movement dedicated to French families. This meeting was the start of the American Christian Family Movement—CFM.

At Prague, the American Catholics and other moderates defended the "center" but were overmatched by leftists operating on their home turf and positioning themselves as those capable of holding off obstacle to a revival of Fascism. The draft constitution presented by the Communists was adopted with only minor changes, and their platform became the IUS agenda. They also claimed leadership and staff positions. This experience convinced the American delegation that the United States could not participate well in such affairs without national student organization representing all American students.

The question as to why they should participate at all may not have even occurred to them. In Europe, where social change had to go through the State, student political activism was almost a necessity because students had free time. Why American students should have been activists rather than sticking to their books is not clear, although Putz was convinced that education should be practical. Putz later would comment ironically on society's readiness to listen to inexperienced students while contemptuously dismissing retired elderly with far more wisdom and knowledge.

The American delegation arranged for a preparatory conference at the University of Chicago in 1946. In the interim, the Prague Four united two national Catholic student groups into the Joint Committee for Student Action and recruited delegates from Catholic institutions and from Newman Clubs at secular universities. Fighting against Catholic reluctance to participate in secular or ecumenical efforts, they succeeded: more than 150 Catholic students attended the Chicago conference. Punctiliously observing correct protocol, the convention was successful. The delegates called overwhelmingly for the creation of a National Student Association (NSA) and elected a committee to organize a constitutional convention at the University of Wisconsin, where, in the following August, the association was born.

For the next 20 years, the NSA grew rapidly in numbers, influence and variety of services. But in the mid-1960s, it encountered the cultural tsunami of the New Left and became internally divided. As the progressives jumped ship, NSA became a counterweight to the New Left and thus attracted the attentions of the FBI and CIA, which wanted to use it to gather intelligence and promote resistance. When these activities were exposed, much of NSA's membership resigned and many colleges severed ties with it. NSA never recovered.

For all its dramatics, the NSA was only a sideshow for Catholic Action. While the Prague Four were launching the NSA, Putz was busy organizing Young Christian Students (YCS) at Notre Dame and throughout the country, both in colleges and high schools. His "can do" spirit echoed the nation's as it turned from war to peace. Putz saw Notre Dame as the best testing ground for YCS. There he had the standing to attract resources, and the earlier activities of Catholic Action had prepared the ground. After receiving leadership training and instruction in the Catholic Workers' Youth Organization (JOC) inquiry method, students became campus leaders, identified unmet student needs and reformed campus institutions.

Immediately after leaving Prague, Putz took the Catholic delegates to a Pax Romana convention in Fribourg, Switzerland. For three weeks they observed the Catholic Student World Association in action and talked with students from many European and South American countries, many of whom were deeply involved in the Christian Democratic parties flourishing in Italy and Germany.

So, the Notre Dame YCS adopted as its first project to supply books to European libraries destroyed in the war. A Mardi Gras celebration raised $35,000 for this purpose. It was pooled with another $90,000 from other colleges and sent to the European Relief Agency in Washington, D.C. But the agency bestowed the funds on publishers and wholesalers who cleared their warehouses of outdated textbooks and other rubbish that was useless to libraries. This bitter experience taught YCS that it would have to maintain control of every phase of its future operations. Thereafter, Notre Dame Mardi Gras celebrations became the major source of support for a new student government.

Putz was determined to make YCS a national movement. He organized a leadership forum at Notre Dame that instructed scores of Catholic Action leaders from across the U.S. in the details of YCS. New YCS groups sprang up in other schools. Rosary College, outside Chicago, hosted a three-week meeting dedicated to YCS. Representatives from Europe and Canada explained their programs to clergy and students from hundreds of campuses and parishes. Before long, YCS became the national movement Putz had envisioned. Strong YCS organizations appeared in scores of Catholic colleges, such as Marquette, St. Ambrose, and St. Theresa.

An order of teaching sisters then asked Putz to help in bringing YCS into their high schools and grade schools. He and the Notre Dame YCS responded with a series of "Plan of Action" booklets aimed at strengthening apostolates in elementary schools. They organized study weeks at Notre Dame to train lay and religious teachers. Over 500 teachers attended. Other YCS cells sprang up in parishes, usually under the impetus of a priest or sister as chaplain. This is how Fr. Leo Trese became involved in Detroit. Meanwhile, Monsig. Hillenbrand and Fr. John Egan, Fr. Vincent Giese, Fr. Dennis Geaney and Fr. Bill Quinn were expanding YCW into a significant presence in Chicago. (Author's note: An early and long-time active member, Mary Irene Zotti, has chronicled the Chicago YCW in an absorbing book called A *Time of Awakening: The Young Christian Worker*.) Nevertheless, Putz was deliberately shut out of YCW in Chicago and increasingly more involved with YCS. He wrote in a 1962 note that the Chicago clergy saw YCW as a preserve for strictly secular and local priests, so Putz could never penetrate its inner circle.

The effort to organize YCS in residence halls was difficult and at first met with indifference, even after Putz recruited hall chaplains to perform chaplain service for YCS. After six months the first hall was organized, and as the results became evident the little movement spread to the other halls and became the strongest student group on the campus. YCS at Notre Dame had two goals: to identify services that students needed, and to find sources of funds to perform them. Both goals were fulfilled when YCS president Jim Cunningham had the idea of organizing a used-textbook exchange. Large commercial dealers earned huge sums by buying up used books for pennies and reselling them the next semester for dollars. The Book Exchange (BX) paid more and charged less for used texts than commercial dealers, but could retain a 10 percent service fee for itself. Everyone but the commercial dealers came out ahead. The students who staffed the BX earned enough to defray their tuition costs, and YCS used much of its share to spread YCS across the country and to help transform student government at Notre Dame.

After the war, Catholic Action shifted its focus from the campus to the city and from men to women. Fr. Putz and CA president Cunningham helped to start a YCW house in South Bend to serve female office workers. When students vacated the campus for the summer, Putz plunged into the Catholic Worker operation run by Julian Pleasants, a YCS charter member, and by another friend. It fed and clothed 40 or more homeless men at a time on the second floor above a pharmacy. Putz talked and ate with the homeless men and tried to restore their self-respect and sense of purpose. There he also exchanged ideas with Dorothy Day and her associate, Peter Maurin, and with Willis Nutting, a future coordinator of a later Putz project. (Author's note: President O'Hara considered Day a Communist and for a while banned her from the campus. Two decades later Notre Dame gave her its highest award, the Laetare Medal.) Bishops, ominously, were less enthusiastic about the lay youth movements. They were asked to issue mandates to YCW and YCS, but they hardly knew what YCS was. Bishop Noll of the diocese including South Bend asked Putz to draft a mandate, which Noll signed blindly. A bookstore far ahead of its time was opened in South Bend by Catholic Actionists; named the Aquinas Library, it sold the latest theology and imported high quality religious art from Europe. There YCS started a publishing company named Apostolate Press to publish translations of major works and to promote liturgical reforms that achieved great influence with the Second Vatican Council two decades later.

Putz was short (five feet, six inches tall) and stockily built, and from his early youth seems to have been afflicted by a vision problem that caused one of his eyes to look in a different direction from the other. Because he wore thick corrective lenses and was not physically well coordinated, he was an "awful" driver, but he refused to admit it. He drove fast, like a German, and would cut the angles on sharp corners, even to driving up on the grass. People were terrified to get in a car with him. In conjunction with his lack of affectation, his vision problem made him slightly comical and disarming. Behaving as a confidante, he could slip under a person's radar in a wink. Agreeing with Putz on some innocuous point, one would suddenly be at the head of a project. As one friend said at a memorial dinner after Putz's death, "Just as you can't say no to Jesus, you could never say no to Putz." To which a Rabbi had replied, "I say no to Jesus all the time, but I still couldn't say no to Putz."

Putz was not the most gifted person on the campus, but his talents were what the new Catholic Action (CA) movement most needed, and his leadership of it makes him in a way the most important cleric or priest who has ever worked in the United States — if CA was what he and it said it was. His friends call him gregarious, but he ever maintained a "germanic" reserve and was never a hail-fellow well-met. Eugene Geissler says he was not a "friendly" person and there was not much American "fun" in him. Nor was he even a one-on-one kind of person, but he shone in groups because ideas poured out of him and he had a broad outlook. He was easy to talk to and a great raconteur, full of interesting stories and always abreast or ahead of the curve. He saw lay people as his equals without losing his appreciation for his clerical state, but he did not think the latter made him more Christian. Those who knew him in the early years all use two adjectives to describe him: charismatic and visionary. Some even use the word "magic." It is difficult at this distance to pinpoint why. Those qualities did not work upon large groups, but on individuals and small groups they produced astounding results. He took huge delight in bringing people together to talk about ideas, with a practical slant. He was a born networker and facilitator, always bringing to others' homes visitors with unusual gifts or experience. During a discussion he would recognize a better way something could be done, and would say to almost anyone, the situation needs to be changed, you can do it, God wants it done, and you will be happy doing it. Hundreds, even thousands, found this message irresistible. Sustained discussion of Great Issues, including religious issues, is uncommon among lay folk, for various reasons. And to discuss secular issues in light of Christian faith seemed a breach of etiquette, if not of "separation." He would get people not only to talk about such things but to think about solutions. And he went further, saying they had both a right and a duty to act on a solution — and that was unheard of.

A nun with whom he returned to Chicago from a meeting in St. Louis gives an example of his visionary quality. Bad weather caused their plane to circle for some time above the Chicago airport, and the terrified woman gripped the arms of her seat with white knuckles. Putz began talking to her about the great future he foresaw for aviation in the Chicago area. She turned to him and gaped. He was always looking past or through the present to a better possibility.

People thought Putz put great trust in them and saw in them a power or potential that no one else grasped half so well. (If CA was to succeed in the U.S., the laity had to sign on and there was no way to compel them.) An early collaborator, Vince Giese, wrote then that Putz "knows with an almost uncanny sensitivity what kind of project or group a young, potential apostle is cut out for" and that this talent could "work marvelous psychological transformations in his leaders."

His influence with lay Catholics seems to have had three sources. The early formative experiences with the laity in France called out and strengthened certain aspects of his personality. And he brought from Europe a unique package: a streamlined and simple method forged through years of hard experience. Fr. Hesburgh thought the Inquiry method smacked of French peculiarities, but it worked. Putz knew how to get a discussion rolling and how to aim it. His idea was that lay people could arrive at a real solution, latent in their give and take, by working together as a unit. As Putz would reaffirm (almost uniquely) in his later years, the intellect is key to the experience of community, for it is mainly through common mental activity that people best come together. The third element was his curious elan. The sentence he adopted as his motto should be engraved on his tomb: "A person who loves is deeply committed, sincerely happy, and always in trouble."

A Catholic Action woman friend of over fifty years, Reggie Weissert, was first dragged by her husband to a Christian Family Movement meeting in the late 1940s. Disliking the discussions, and one of the men in the group, she wanted to quit, but her husband remained enthusiastic. She saw Putz as cold and remote, and was "greatly unimpressed" by him, because during the meeting at which she first laid eyes on him he sat at the back of the room, said nothing and seemed to doze. At the meeting's end she was astonished when he repeated back to the participants, almost verbatim, every point they had made. She resolved to make the best of a bad bargain and began to pay attention to the discussions. Gradually she became interested, then caught fire. Putz, she says almost ruefully, "changed my life."

A later close Putz associate, Sr. Edith Daley, c.s.c., says that what impressed her most was that he respected people's gifts, however small, and praised them without flattery. (He liked her common sense.) Unlike most others in the diocese, he was selective in what he would praise. He could mobilize people as gifted as himself and generate enthusiasm, because they were often bored in their ruts and wanted to do something different, and he could convince them that they would achieve something important, indeed that they had a mission.

Early in its career, Putz's specialized Catholic Action group at Notre Dame, called Young Christian Students (YCS), began agitating for an organization that would replace it: a strong student government. By the end of the 1950s the student government had largely displaced YCS in the consciousness of students. This was the first example of another Putz characteristic: his readiness to let go of his own creations for a higher purpose. People have put different interpretations on this but it may have a simple explanation. He never fully bought into a program because his program was the process and not any specific objective. His goal was to get the laity activated and going through the proper steps, because he had learned in France that real solutions are elusive, unpredictable and found only by addressing the problems in the right way. Even an abstractly great answer is wrong if not discovered through the correct process. (Again, this contradicts most modern wisdom.) It is not simply that he trusted the laity to find answers but that only they could really find them. The hierarchy expected the laity to blunder and fail, and insisted on firm control. Putz's attitude better mirrored that of an equally "unrealistic" Jesus.

Putz's routine practice could not have departed further from the statutes promulgated in the 1950s at the Fifth Synod of the Diocese for Fort Wayne, which encompassed South Bend. They included two advisories: that social visits by priests with laity should serve some pastoral purpose and not extend past 11 PM, and that priests' visits to laity in parishes other than their own should be justified by special occasions and could not be countenanced as a regular practice. The rules aimed to preserve a wall between clergy and the lesser order of laity.

The first project YCS undertook at Notre Dame was to address the campus "negro" problem. Imagine the administration's discomfort. It couldn't claim that Putz and YCS were wrong, but why must they be so untimely? Nor was a stronger student government something it would contemplate with undiluted joy. Putz was a trouble-maker; he rocked the boat and was making himself a marked man.

Putz was as yet the only person in America with his precise vision of how the Church should operate, but he thought it was eminently orthodox and correct, and European CA had schooled him to fight like a tiger (although with all charity) for what he thought. Where was the line between principle and effrontery? It was a matter of temperament and judgment. People with whom Putz needed to work on routine administrative projects often found him "not easy to work with," for he tended to insist on his own priorities over the institution's. To succeed, how could he have done otherwise?

But he paid the price early and often. A turning point in Catholic Action's evolution in the U.S. arrived when some of the CA leaders at Notre Dame bought an 80-acre tract of land as a community. Five of the families helped three of them build houses on the site, on which some are still living. Did they ever consider living together in the same house, or forming a commune? Forces were pulling each family in a different direction. A member, Jim Cunningham, says one of the negative forces was Putz's "heavy-handed" methods. He was "a man of contradictions": a champion of lay initiative and leadership who was "strongly directive." He was anxious to get CA running but lacked the patience to be consistent. Cunningham thought a strong authoritarian streak in German culture surfaced in Putz's own character. And as Geissler says, no sooner did he know you than he wanted to use you. He impulsively came up with new ideas that he tried to impose on the group, and once you bit, he fully expected you to finish the job. Geissler says Putz's great talent was for starting new projects. When one was running, he went on to another. He was no control freak, at least at first; as soon as others took initiative he stepped back.

His congregation generally saw him at least as "authentic." Some of the wives became unhappy with his strong influence on their husbands, although all recognized his genius as a builder. The little community never really jelled.

Marty McLaughlin is more pointed. He calls Putz "an aggressive, even arbitrary, democrat." When he later became the rector of a seminary, Putz's first step was to tell the seminarians that by the next day they must have written a constitution. Once he had decided what should be done, McLaughlin says, he was not receptive to your version; once he had made up his mind, if you disagreed with him you were gone. One generally didn't object because what he was doing was right. "He made us do things and take responsibility." McLaughlin says had he not met Putz his life would have been much different. He would not have become concerned with social justice, nor stayed for a Ph.D., nor married his wife. Putz's influence on him was entirely good. He was one of the few real personalities on the Notre Dame campus and he knew how to work the system and did it often.

An Iowa priest named Dave Hogan remembers an example of Putz's intrepidity. Putz invited Betty Snyder, head of the Chicago branch of the Baroness Catherine de Hueck Doherty's Friendship House (which worked on racial justice) to speak on the Notre Dame campus, and Putz tabbed student Hogan to introduce her. But Hogan had to seek permission from a redoubtable prefect of discipline, a Fr. Kehoe, to use university facilities. When Hogan hesitated, Putz rebuked him and told him to put his faith in the Holy Spirit. Kehoe readily gave permission. In her talk Snyder blistered the Church for avoiding a strong stand for racial justice. Hogan said the speech "opened my eyes," and he asked to spend a week at the Chicago Friendship House, in a black area. Putz encouraged Hogan's desire to become a parish priest because priests who really knew what the laity needed and could help them become agents of change were rare. Hogan remained a strongly "activist" priest for the next 50 years. Many similarly trained by YCS went on to be leaders in politics, law, the media and other fields.

Putz's letters are impressive. They are concentrated and pithy, deal deftly with delicate political and relational tensions and exude wisdom. And his writings and talks exhibit insight into practical problems. When he read theory he noticed first of all its practical implications. He seemed to admire the human aspect of Jesus more than the divine, and noted that the carpenter Joseph did not make mainly furniture nor houses, but yokes for animals, and they had to fit. This threw light on his son's remark that "my yoke is easy and my burden light."

The Notre Dame Catholic Action group, as it first styled itself, was far from the only lay movement in the country. The U.S. Church was a seething cauldron of lay activism. Dorothy Day's Catholic Worker movement jostled with Fr. Lord's Solidarity Catholic Action summer schools, Msgr. Ligutti's rural movement, the catechist movement promoted by Bishop O'Hara of Kansas City, de Hueck Doherty's Friendship House (racial justice) and Madonna House, the Grail, the Catholic Youth Organization (CYO) of Bishop Shiel (this group was almost as prophetic as Catholic Action, for it was the first in the U.S. to support lay Catholics mainly in their secular roles), and several others. (The astonishing ferment presents a stark contrast to today's American Catholicism.) But Catholic Action was the only kind that put lay persons in the lead. Putz explained how in 1936 the French Catholic youth movement had adopted the JOC model and applied the "like to like" principle to all of its activities, forming the Young Christian Students (JEC), Young Christian Farmers (JAC), Young Christian University Students (JUC), and Young Christian Mariners (JMC). He saw this division as suited to the American scene as well.

CA, Putz said, is a work "in the flesh" — neither purely religious nor clerical, but a lay movement to the world. The scandal of the 20th century was the loss of the working masses to the socialist and communist movements; indeed, all of the institutions of the modern world (he wrote) grew up outside of Christian influence. The laity must reshape them according to the mind of Christ so that people's souls and salvation will not be actually endangered by contact with the temporal order. A family must be an apostolic unit in the neighborhood, determined to radiate its influence and bring about a fundamental change, not only in this or that other family but in the whole institutional character of families in the district, or block, or state, or world. And the same for all professions in their spheres: lawyers, lawmakers, doctors, journalists, employers, workers. The objective is nothing less than the complete renewal of the world.

But how was the family supposed to do this? How could a single family, or even a group of families, change the institutional character of families even in the neighborhood? To solve the family's problems, it was not enough to diagnose the problem precisely, if this could be done. Families had to find a way to combine or would remain forever on defense.

Hillenbrand in Chicago heard of Putz's activity and experience, and invited him, too, to address the Chicago deacons. At this lecture Hillenbrand and his group for the first time learned and appeared to grasp the real principles of the JOC movement: the necessity and reasons for lay leadership and control, the focus on action, the strategic centrality of the cell or group, the merely advisory role of the priest, and so forth. Nothing like this, Hillenbrand realized, had yet appeared on American soil. With Cardinal Stritch's support, a mild form of Catholic Action began to take root in Chicago. But it had to be cautious and respectful of the "liberal" Stritch's prerogatives. Chicago's YCW cells were dominated by priests, and dynamic priests like Egan gravitated toward other work, such as cooperation with Saul Alinsky. Putz wanted to be involved with YCW, but he wrote in a 1962 note that the Chicago clergy wanted to preserve YCW in Chicago for secular and local priests, and he could never penetrate its inner circle.

World War II claimed many of the Young Christian Workers, but as Notre Dame became a virtual army barracks, Catholic Action thrived. Frs. Howard Kenna and Charles Sheedy formed three Catholic Action groups among the Navy and Marine men billeted at the campus, and several of the young officers then established similar groups on ships. The third president of YCS at Notre Dame was Mark McGrath, who soon entered the Holy Cross order and later as archbishop of Panama became the leader of the Latin American Catholic hierarchy during the turbulent 1960s. He was the main figure at the famous (or infamous) Medellin conference, which set a new course ("a preferential option for the poor") for the Church in Latin America. Putz and YCS leader Jim Cunningham helped to open a YCW house for girls working in South Bend offices, and Catholic Action groups organized at South Bend's Leeper Park dances and socials open to the city's blacks, to the mayor's delight. Not long afterwards Putz and YCS pressured the executive vice president, Fr. John Cavanaugh, to recruit and welcome blacks to the campus. He demurred, saying that the 400 southern students would rebel. So YCS surveyed the southerners on the campus, and all but two, who were about to withdraw, supported the YCS initiative. The university still held out, until the Navy sent a black sailor to Notre Dame for training. After the war, Fr. Putz and YCS found this young veteran and urged him to apply for admission to a degree program. He did, and the university acquiesced, finally ending its color barrier. Fr. Putz and YCS had launched a local civil rights movement 20 years before blacks did.

Louis Putz brought into the United States not only the name of special-ized Catholic Action but its objectives and structures. For him CA was an organized group apostolate aimed at social institutions to make them and the culture more hospitable to Christian faith. The goal of conversions was central. But Catholic Action encountered in the U.S. a cultural situation that was very different from Europe's.

Father Patrick Beyton with Father Putz and movie stars Roddy McDowell and Ann Blyth

Roddy McDowell

McDowall was a child actor who continued his career successfully into adulthood, notably in four of the five original Planet of the Apes movies (1968–1973) and the TV series that followed. Other film appearances included Cleopatra (1963), It! (1966), The Poseidon Adventure (1972), Dirty Mary, Crazy Larry (1974), Class of 1984 (1982), Fright Night (1985) and Overboard (1987). McDowall interest in film preservation led to the preserving of Cleopatra (1963). Dowall served for years in various capacities on the Board of Governors of the Academy of Motion Picture Arts and Sciences, the organization that presents the Oscar. He was elected President of the Academy Foundation the year he died.

Ann Blyth

A leading lady of 1940's /1950's Musicals and Dramas. She began her career at 15. In 1944 she appears in four Hollywood Musicals with musical partner Donald O'Connor. 1945: Receives an Academy Award Nomination for her role as the disturbing, ill-behaved daughter in the movie Mildred Pierce. Some Best Movies: Mr Peabody and the Mermaid, The Great Caruso.

"The Gospel has not changed nor the need to
proclaim it. What has changed and is changing always
is the world."

The Modern Apostle by Louis J. Putz, CSC (1957) p. 23

Aquinas, a book store started by Putz
(standing on far right)

Chapter 4
Publisher and Promoter

Success in its early small ventures prompted Fides Press, a little publishing operation headquartered at Aquinas Bookstore, to set its sights on higher goals. Putz began to recruit to it a talented and dedicated staff ready to work for peanuts and the joy of an exciting and demanding mission with high stakes. The collection of secular saints and survivalists was up to the challenge Putz set, and they made Fides the conduit for the ideas Putz had encountered in Europe, and in general for the mobilization of the Catholic laity.

Meanwhile, YCS's successful promotion of a strong student government had the unexpected effect of all but killing off YCS at Notre Dame. However YCS under Putz's tutelage flourished in grade and high schools and became a massive apostolate for him and some new associates. Putz's efforts toward educating and training laity continued through Fides Press. Partly as a result of his work with the Marriage Institute, Putz was involved, arguably as its founder, with a group that became the most successful of Catholic Action's progeny: the Christian Family Movement, an organization that encapsulated all of the problems and issues endemic to Catholic Action in the United States.

Like those who ran the Aquinas bookstore, Fides staffers had to learn the business as they went. Starting without capital, the venture was from the start an exercise in faith. Soon learning that pre-publication book were huge, they had to seek funding. The prospects for attracting investment capital were nil, so Putz set about to secure loans and approached, among others, the "ordinaries" of the dioceses of Fort Wayne/South Bend and Chicago, Bishop Pursley and Cardinal Stritch, as well as the Archbishop of Boston, Richard Cushing, and the Bishop of Worcester, John W. Wright. Putz, the supposed radical, sought financing from bishops to spread his message, and his success shows they all viewed him as orthodox. The loans enabled Fides to publish books and steadily expand its list of publications.

Over the years Fides received solicited and unsolicited advice from a host of real and would-be publishing gurus. The regional provincial superior of the Holy Cross congregation offered advice to Putz that criticized his use of personnel talent. Faulting Fides for attempting to operate without capital and under debt, they could not understand its mission. But many friends who knew what was going on made real sacrifices of small funds, such as J. Peter Grace's personal foundation, which sent in $1,000 yearly.

As Fides launched book after book, its need for marketing funds kept it under perpetual strain. Its first solution was to publish a new theological library for which it solicited advance subscribers. This venture could have ruined the firm, but for a while it held off the financial wolf. The next solution was to enter the Catholic textbook business in order to generate sufficient volume to smooth out the financial hills and valleys for the more commercial line. That, too, generated great concern among Fides' friends, including a director. Reviews of the Fides files suggest that the real problem was that Fides expanded so quickly that each solution incurred higher costs. But Fides became a bellwether and trendsetter in religious publishing by importing much of Europe's best writing and theology. Larger firms scrambled to keep up as Fides became known as an innovative high quality publisher.

Bishop Pursley and Cardinal Stritch fretted over Fides's orthodoxy. Stritch would write Putz notes that numerous books—for example, Fides' very influential book, *Catholic Church*, USA, to which Putz contributed a preface and which was read avidly in the Vatican—had crossed over the line. Yet, the patrons continued their support, knowing that Fides was performing an important task exceptionally well. It had become the main propaganda arm of Catholic Action. They would have preferred that Fides make money, but it would have been far less influential. The operation perpetually teetered on the brink as the books poured out: wonderful books of theology, spirituality, social commentary and every related subject.

At a meeting near Detroit, Fr. Leo Trese asked Putz if he would be interested in a manuscript Trese had composed, called *Many Are One*. The book became a best-seller, Fides's first. More than a million copies were distributed. Nine other popular Trese books followed. The next summer, Putz, along with editor Vince Giese and two others, visited European religious publishers, authors, young progressive theologians and leaders of Catholic Action. His German origins, experience in France and fluency in five languages opened many doors, and gained Fides the right to publish original manuscripts and English translations of several masterpieces. Prominent among the acquisitions were the pastoral letters of the great Emmanuel Cardinal Suhard, who had a huge influence on the future Pope John XXIII. The first of Suhard's letters, *The Church Today*, had an equally huge impact on American Catholics and was another Fides best-seller. Works by Romano Guardini and Henri Delubac followed. Fides was becoming a publishing powerhouse and a strong voice for the reforms that Vatican Council II would adopt a few years later. A good publisher needs three qualities and Putz had exhibited all of them: great energy, a delicate sensitivity to trends, and a strong intellectuality. Putz wanted to bring the New Theology from Europe to the United States and saw a theology-oriented intellect as essential to Catholic Action's goal of social reconstruction. Fides helped to prepare American Catholics for Vatican II's reforms, but its main purpose was to make American Catholics operate in secular society as Catholics.

With the help of another close associate, Harriet Kroll, Putz became swamped by the YCS apostolate in grade schools and junior high schools, to which he provided inspirational and spiritual materials, partly in the form of monthly inserts to Fr. Frank Gartland, C.S.C., editor of CB and CM, (Garland's newsletters were called *Catholic Boy* and *Catholic Miss*). Conducted by Notre Dame's Catholic Action for teachers and nuns, they had generated a strong interest and market for continuing programs, which Putz used Fides to supply, and he apparently wrote most of the densely packed articles. They had a moralizing slant but showed that Putz had thought much about the practical issues in students' lives.

In retrospect, the publishing to the grade-school and high-school markets, seemingly the least of his enterprises, made a huge and growing claim on his energies, and it may have had a larger impact on the Church than all of Catholic Action's other activities. In a talk he gave to religious leaders of school-based Catholic Action, he said that in the prior 100 years the American Church's task had been to build churches, schools and parishes. Its task in the next 100 years would be to build a Christian society, with schools playing a major role. He saw their mission, apart from developing the mind, as to provide an example and experience in Christian living. Starting in college was too late, and would never reach those who didn't attend college. He fretted about the weakness in the educational system and wanted to focus on concrete life.

Throughout the 1950s, Louis Putz was up to his ears in work for CFM, YCS and Fides. Today disciples from that era consider it to have been the most challenging, educational, and growth filled time of their lives. Many yearn for it to be available for themselves and their offspring today. Fortified by these positive values and talents, Catholic Action members were well prepared and eager to help implement their directives of Vatican II and its resultant wealth of documents. The parochial resistance they encountered in numerous cases caused some of the strongest and most highly motivated individuals to become thwarted by the gigantic amounts of effort required to carry on lay initiatives in their parishes while at the same time continuing in the civic commitments. It consisted of facilitating encounters and engagement among lay people. The most intense laboratory of lay activism, probably anywhere in the world, during that decade was Chicago, and yet most of that activity also has been lost. In 1992, Ed Marciniak (he stood tall in a group, among many others, who were disciples of Monsignor Reynold Hillenbrand, a charismatic advocate of lay action for social justice) acclaimed a book entitled *This Confident Church: Catholic Leadership and Life in Chicago*, written by Steven M. Avella (Notre Dame, Indiana: University of Notre Dame Press, 1992) as the first book ever to suggest the scope of lay activity in the city. Marciniak noted however that it was written entirely from the episcopacy's point of view and ignored much of the most significant activity (such as that of Chicago Inter-Student Catholic Action—CISCA—which funneled huge numbers of recruits into all the branches of Catholic Action). Lay Catholics pioneered many partnerships between laity and clergy, and Hillenbrand's priests facilitated the process from the other side. In their day those priests seemed radical. (Author's note: Avella's book offers compelling portraits of great leaders, such as Bishop Shiel and Monsignor Hillenbrand, and Frs. Cantwell, Egan and Quinn.)

Marciniak was right. In those days, the American Catholic Church had a seething, boiling underground.In South Bend, Louis Putz participated in many discussions conducted in the living room of the Weisserts, the Krolls, and the Peraltas. He was said to haunt the Aquinas Bookstore, a cauldron of lay activism that lent and sold books, and sponsored concerts, lectures, retreats, conferences and an army of small organizations, including the press. The bookstore organizers wrote that it would have been impossible without Putz. Bishop Noll too was anxious about "outreach," so he had his auxiliary, Bishop Pursley, pressure Aquinas Bookstore to open a Catholic Information Center. It did, and it was a failure. Thereafter, Noll thought he was the source of the bookstore's success. A picture shows Putz standing with the "rosary priest," Patrick Peyton, movie star Ann Blyth and teen-age heartthrob Roddie McDowell after some radio broadcast on a spiritual subject. Throughout the 1940s and well into the 1950s Putz was a force in (and some insist the founder of) South Bend Legion of Mary. Many inquired as to Putz's motives, since the legion did not specifically attempt to change society. However, Putz became involved because the Legion of Mary was dedicated to evangelization, a prime Catholic Action concern. Putz could always be found in Fides's office, at CFM meetings and projects, as well as behind half a dozen YCS projects on the Notre Dame campus, including student government.

How Putz kept track of projects is difficult to guess. Madeleva Sullivan Peyton, who had assisted Father Putz in editing the grade school YCS materials, brought specialized Catholic Action to California in his urgings. The Christian Family Movement went from strength to strength, forging its own path, but its independence put Putz in a constant bind with the Church bureaucracy. For example, the director of the Family Life Bureau of the National Catholic Welfare Conference (NCWC—an organization under the American bishops) reminded Bishop Noll in 1953 that his Episcopal moderator had never approved of the "so-called Christian Family Movement" because it had always ignored the Family Life Bureau. The bureau was controlled by the bishops; the CFM by lay people. It was Putz's unenviable task to ease these tensions and to explain to the Church's Nolls what Catholic Action was doing and why. The National Federation of Catholic College Students (NFCCS) was also doubtful of Putz's "specialized" version of Catholic Action and preferred the types more amenable to episcopal control. Putz negotiated a modus vivendi. His excellent letters and good relations with ordinaries were crucial to specialized Catholic Action's survival.

In a 1954 article ("Adult Education—Family Style") for a YCS publication named *Anima*, Putz wrote that large families were CA's best recruiting grounds because they knew how to depend on each other. He lamented society's constant discouragements to large families (e.g., bachelors being paid the same as fathers of large families) and called for a European-type family allowance to smooth out the inequities. Catholic education also imposed an onerous budget item on Catholic families, and he saw CFM as a major part of the solution. For Putz, the 1950s were the best and worst of times; his rapidly expanding undertakings made his burden almost insupportable. He was embroiled in constant financial and political struggles of Fides, campus crusades (strong student government, and racial equity) of YCS, the development of YCS in grade and high schools, and perpetual back-stage maneuvering to make specialized Catholic Action comprehensible to the institutional Church.

With its growing importance and success, Fides was invited to move to a multi-mission center at 21 West Superior Street in Chicago that housed several other groups: Fr. Daniel Cantwell's Catholic Interracial

Council, John Egan's Cana Conference, and *Work*, a labor-oriented newspaper edited by Marciniak and Bob Senser. Vince Giese became editorial director of Fides; Katie O'Connor, Putz's long-time associate who earlier had founded a house for single working girls in South Bend, became business manager before Bill McCullough and Vince's brother, Clarence, a graduate of the Art Institute of Chicago, was the art director. All were now full-time low-salaried employees, a far cry from the early days when Giese worked for $25 a week and Fr. Louis worked for free. While still teaching at Notre Dame and directing half a dozen Catholic Action groups, Putz continued as Fides's executive director and guiding light, securing valuable publishing contracts with European houses, such as Herder & Herder in Germany and Editions du Cerf in Paris.

When the Vatican ordered the suppression of Yves Congar's book, Reform in the Church, Putz had the idea of recasting Congar's ideas in magazine format and issuing them serially. Thus American readers were able to consider Congar's views. (Author's note: Congar, along with Frs. Danielou and DeLubac, all silenced by the Vatican Congregation of Doctrine under Garrigou-LaGrange, whom Jacques Maritain criticized sharply, later was raised to Cardinal by Pope Paul VI.) It was the six-volume "Theological Library," a sort of summa of the New Theology, written by eminent young French theologians, that could have sunk the firm. But the firm found additional financing, completed the project and survived. It was not so lucky with another project, a four-volume religious text for high school classes.

Fides's quarter-century career described an arc that peaked at about half a million dollars in sales in 1966. In the upswing, its markets slowly became mainly institutional: Catholic schools and CCD classes conducted for Catholic students of public schools. The textbook projects stabilized Fides for a while, although not by reducing its debt. Fides received a premonitory warning in 1965 when sales of apostolic books suddenly dropped sharply while demand for sociological titles soared. The downswing that started in 1966 had two main causes. The external cause was a drastic change in the market. Catholic schools began to close as nuns and priests became laicized and lay teachers took over (they didn't want books, but "teaching aids"); meanwhile, denominational lines blurred and the emphasis in religion shifted from institutional expressions and practice to more purely human factors. Whether this was theological progress or regression still seems difficult to say; it may have been both. But the result was that Fides's "backlist"—the old profitable "reliables" on which it depended for half its sales—became obsolete overnight and reduced the firm's cash flow drastically, so that it could not rebuild the list quickly. Fides never recovered financially from this sudden blow; from then on it swam underwater, as many of its larger competitors disappeared.

That doesn't mean Fides could not have succeeded in the new era, but one difficulty was lethal. It was mal-organization within the firm, and it seems to have stemmed from Putz's control. He saw Fides as a Catholic Action apostolate, and expected the staff to work together as a team—for a long time. But lacking business experience, Putz did not understand the organizational requirements of a business. Fides desperately needed clear lines of authority and accountability, and a staff motivated by intrinsic and extrinsic rewards. Instead, Putz assigned people to specialized tasks but gave them little authority and made them work as a committee. Unable to derive satisfaction from personal achievement, the committee bogged down in interminable discussions. Only Putz could resolve problems, which he often did by edict.

Jim Cunningham was employed at Fides in its early years in South Bend and remained a director until the end. He saw that Putz tended to take control of decisions and agendas, especially when others showed any uncertainty. He found elusive the line between expressing and imposing his strong views, and when preparing someone for a meeting, he would lay out in advance everything that needed to be done. Putz was deriving loads of satisfaction from his work, at the expense of the others. He did not heed his own message enough by trusting his people, whom he had asked to perform a virtual miracle, and they came within a hair of doing it. If they never went over the hump, he could have been the main cause. His role in Fides became as anomalous as Reynold Hillenbrand's in the Christian Family Movement, but for Putz, who understood Catholic Action much better, there was less excuse.

He finally heeded his provincial's urgings and appointed the sales director to be overall manager (but this was his unilateral decision). The manager had been an unsuccessful car dealer and turned out to be incapable of confrontations. By then Putz was "Mr. Fides" to the world and everyone inside the firm knew it. Religious publishing, it had turned out, was an almost incredibly complex business. Most businesses have two or three crucial "success factors," but this one seemed to have ten. For example, most successful publishers in the field had large capital and accepted only established writers because that was most profitable. But Fides, without capital, could not pay such writers and had to search out new talent constantly with more than usual rates of success. It did but this was only one of its continuous problems.

Still, a heartrending letter of resignation that Vince Giese, the most talented editor, wrote to Putz in 1961 shows that Putz should have bitten the bullet. Giese wrote that he felt stifled at Fides and unable to grow. He thought much of the staff was dead wood. He was also alarmed: he had dedicated 11 years of his life to Fides and seemed to have nothing to show for it. He knew it would be difficult to begin a new career somewhere else, but he had do it (he entered a seminary). The letter, strongly suggesting that the interaction inside the firm had ossified, should have been a wake-up call to Fr. Putz, but he appears to have brushed it aside. Yet he remained fully active in the firm only for another four years, and missed the chance to build a great organization. At the end of those four years, he was trapped: creditors said they would call in all loans if he left. So he had to stay on as a figurehead, watching the firm bleed to death.

Thus occurred another of the tragedies suffered by Catholic Action. Putz never suspected that the greatest role Fides might have performed could have been not just as a unique type of publisher, which it was, but as a unique type of business, operated as much by and for its own people as for investors or the general public. What could Putz have done? There were several possibilities. Instead of paying the staff tiny salaries, he could have let them divide up any surplus according to a formula they worked out themselves. Since Fides in effect had no payable shareholders, nothing really stood in the way. That step would have given them a powerful material incentive to make the business successful, in addition to the incentive they already had to make it survive. He could have insisted on clear individual challenges and accountability not only to him but to each other. Individuals could have been permitted and enabled to succeed as professionals and to have paid the price for failure. Finally, and arguably the most important, he could have tried to make the "little group" into a real community. Materially, it was communal, since members were paid according to need and not contribution or performance. (The company also gave books away to customers—libraries, prisons—that could not pay.) But it was not true that any member could at any time become a leader; Putz was the only leader. So, increasingly after 1961, there was balkanization, lack of communication, turnover, secrecy and a considerable waste of time and energy. An energetic salesman who came on board in 1964 said that the firm needed an inside dictator who really knew what was going on. That might have worked in a conventional firm, but Fides's staff was working for nothing but ideals. Fides failed the two-part test of real community in one way, much as CFM, as we shall see, failed it in the other.

In taking on so much of the load, Louis Putz overburdened himself needlessly for apart from the debt, other problems hung over Fides for years. The most disturbing was a demand by the IRS for back taxes. Fides was organized as a non-profit in 1947 under a tax code of 1937, which was changed in 1954 to be more stringent with respect to non-profits, but Fides went blithely on unaware. When its textbook project succeeded, the brisk sales triggered a lawsuit by a commercial competitor that claimed that Fides enjoyed an unwarranted exemption from taxes as a not-for-profit corporation when in fact Fides earned profits. The IRS and a court agreed. That itself was not so bad, because Fides earned only small profits. But the IRS wanted to make the ruling retroactive to 1954, and to make Fides pay taxes on all its previous profits. Even worse, it demanded that Fides capitalize rather than expense its plate costs. That step would have raised Fides' reported annual profits by $10,000, and its taxes commensurably. Because of Fides's thin cash reserves, this would have put it out of business. Most vulnerable was the textbook operation, without which Fides probably could not survive. Managers fought the ruling for almost a decade, at a huge expense in time and worry. Fides lost its tax exempt status but avoided paying taxes retroactively.

Costs to Fides were associated with a talented translator who claimed to be a reformed alcoholic. Good translators were in short supply. This man arguably did a fine job for a while, but supposedly "ran wild" when he went to Europe. He then formed a company for which he used Fides's letterhead and then made contradictory "exclusive" partnerships with a host of collaborators from whom he solicited money using Fides's name. When the truth emerged, some collaborators sued Fides, surprising it as much as he had them. The matter dragged on interminably and caused much grief, although no financial loss. Yet another problem was a feisty female religion author who wrote good books but constantly second-guessed the publisher's promotion and distribution. A second sister became a scourge in 1965. Explaining to them the realities of publishing was difficult.

The local Bishop Pursley continued to recognize Putz's gifts and sincerity and remained a strong supporter, even when they disagreed. With Putz as rector of a seminary, and still deeply involved with Fides, Pursley was displeased that Fides published the future dissident Charles Curran, rather than calling in his loans, and he withdrew Putz's permission to serve as censor deputatis. Pursley must have been watching closely, because the Curran book was the only one in a long list that year that was remotely objectionable. Putz wrote Pursley a diplomatic and deferential reply to his protest. This and other letters reveal Putz as a master of diplomacy, and patently honest and sincere. Putz and Pursley later clashed even more dramatically. The dance of Putz with Pursley is one of the interesting aspects of Putz's life.

Fides enjoyed its last bright success with its 1965 book *Seminary Education in a Time of Change*, a collection of essays on the subject by luminaries such as John Tracy Ellis, Adrian L. van Kaam, John L. McKenzie and Robert O. Johann. Putz edited the book (and contributed a chapter) along with his university friend, James Michael Lee, who later operated a religious education publishing firm at a deficit out of his own pocket. This may have been the most influential book ever published by a small Catholic publisher. (Author's note: this is discussed further in Chapter Nine.) Some think that by drawing Putz away from Fides, the book drove a stake into the publisher's heart. But in fact, Putz was lucky the book gave him an excuse to get out, because Fides's organization would drag it down as the problems escalated. Harriet Kroll managed Fides for several years after 1965, but by 1969 it came under full control and ownership (Putz remained nominal chairman) of the salesman mentioned earlier. He purchased the Aquinas bookstore and contributed it to Fides in exchange for personal ownership of most of the company's stock. By then, the organization's structure had become entirely conventional (inefficient) and as the markets continued to change, Fides slipped farther behind. The new managers failed to grasp that the Catholic laity, having turned inward, had robbed Fides of its older market. Its assets were sold in 1976 to the Claretian Fathers, publishers of U.S. *Catholic* magazine, for $40,000, or one quarter of Fides's debts. Many of its creditors came away with only 25 cents on the dollar. Fides disappeared soon thereafter. Nevertheless, nothing can besmirch its memory or achievement. It had been arguably the prime force in Catholic publishing over its first twenty years—crucial years for the Catholic Church.

Below is a Homily from Father Putz.

The Lay Apostolate

The subject for this Sunday's instruction is the lay apostolate. A fitting topic for Pentecost Sunday, the day on which the divine fire bolted like a hurricane from the throne of God into the hearts of men. Aflame with that sacred fire and with our Lord's last command, "Go, teach all nations" still sounding in their ears, the small group of Apostles burst open the doors of the Cenacle with an energetic resolve to tell the world about Christ and His redeeming mission on earth.

On that first Pentecost, the Church chalked up an enrollment of three thousand converts; these, in turn, carried their faith with conviction and enthusiasm to the four corners of the earth. From small beginnings, the Catholic Church rose and developed into a numerous family as the Christian leaven slowly but irresistibly worked its way into the marrow of society, into the masses of the Roman Empire. Peter and Paul were zealous men but even with all their zeal they would have accomplished little had it not been for the help they received from Apollo, Prisca and Aquilla, and a host of other laymen and women who put their time and their means and talents into the balance for Christ. Thus, within a relatively short time the great Roman family of nations was changed from a pagan into a Christian commonwealth.

The Christians of the early Church might well serve us as models. What was the secret of their fervor, of their success in the Christian lay apostolate? Undoubtedly, the answer lies in the sincerity with which they translated the Gospel into their daily life. They were not mere believers, but actors, doers, missionaries, missionaries to their immediate neighborhood. Thus, the slave of the mines converted his fellow miners; the toga-ed Roman worked on his friend of the Forum, and the Roman lady treated her army of slaves as brothers and sisters. "Who among the pagans," asks Tertullian, "would permit his wife to walk through distant streets and to enter the poorest dwellings to visit the brethren? Who would permit them to enter secretly into dungeons for the purpose of kissing the chains of the martyrs? Or participate in eating and drinking, to beg food for the poor?" There are so many snapshots of the Roman lady's apostolate taken from her rounds of charity. No wonder the pagans had to exclaim in sheer admiration, "See how they love one another!?"

What was the motor, the wellspring of this extraordinary zeal of the early Christians? They loved all men because all are children of the one common Father, who makes the sun to shine upon the good and the bad alike; they loved all men because all were saved in the blood of their brother, Jesus Christ. "Whatsoever you do to the least of these my brethren, you shall have done it unto me." With the poor they shared their wealth, with the suffering, their sympathy, with the slave and the social outcast, their roof and hospitality. "All were of one mind and soul," says St. Luke in the Acts of the Apostles, "nor was there any needy among them." No selfish clutch on their wealth for the sake of a certain standard of living or social prestige. Like a mighty flood their charity destroyed class barriers and leveled social distinctions. They did not relegate Christianity to the convent or the priest's rectory.

To be a lay apostle, moreover, you need not necessarily become a social worker or a foreign missionary; you need not be a dynamic orator. You need merely be keenly alive to the needs of your neighbor, the neighbor of your immediate environment. Proximus, the Latin word for neighbor, is the man next to you. He is frequently overlooked in our ministrations of charity. He is the man in the ditch whom the priest and the Levite overlooked in the story of the Good Samaritan because they were in a hurry to get home. In our school environment it might be the student who needs our help to understand his lesson or assignment, it might be a delinquent in studies or discipline, it might be a poor fellow who is preyed upon by the vices of laziness and sensuality. Timely reminders, kind advice, a kind word or sympathetic concern might save a broken spirit or otherwise lost soul. Real, effective personal charity makes a man good, patient, not arrogant, not repulsive. It is the master key that will open every heart. It is acquired by a constant doing of little acts of services, a readiness to serve others and sacrifice oneself.

You may know the story of Spike Riley, an American boy in the battle of Guadalcanal. He belonged to a gun mortar crew. There were three boys at his gun when a grenade from a Japanese mortar landed squarely among them. Riley threw himself on the grenade and was nearly blown to pieces. One day when he was well enough to talk, the chaplain asked Riley why he had made this tremendous act of sacrifice. He turned to him and said in a very matter of fact way, "Padre, I had gone to confession and I knew I was ready to die. I wasn't so sure about those other two boys." Spike Riley was a lay apostle. He was ready to lay down his life for his friends. But such an act presupposes many less spectacular acts of service performed in behalf of his soldier friends.

Examples of individual apostolate can undoubtedly be multiplied. Yet, in recent years the Church has found it necessary to organize the lay apostles; the organized lay apostolate is known by the name of Catholic Action. This is the modern layman's great opportunity for the Apostolate. Every Catholic by the grace of Confirmation is given the strength to be a soldier of Christ. Now, a soldier does not primarily fight for himself, but for his country, his fellow countrymen, his sacred rights and principles. The lay apostle of Catholic Action is organized to bring Christ to the world. We need not investigate very deeply modern habits of thought and action to realize that Christ is sadly excluded from everyday life. He is out of education, out of marriage, out of the relationship between a man and his neighbor, between parent and child, between husband and wife; Christ is out of entertainment, out of literature, and out of leisure; Christ is out of private and public life. This is clearly not the normal thing because God should be the center of things if He is the master of the universe. Who will bring Him back to His rightful place in the world? In our complex modern existence, the Church has been assigned a place, a slice of man's life – Sunday. The rest of his life escapes his influence. The layman alone is in daily and hourly touch with the workaday world. He alone can bring Christ back into every phase of life in his own person and in the lives of his fellow worker. That is the reason why the recent Popes have been so insistent on Catholic Action for the layman. Many souls will be lost through little fault of their own, just because they belong to a paganized world where pagan principles hold sway. The need of the Catholic lay leadership is indeed great, it is a desperate need. According to Pope Pius XI, without Catholic Action the world will not be saved. Christ's sacrifice would therefore have been in vain.

Let us ask the Divine Spirit to rise up from out of your ranks of lay leaders, men of wisdom and understanding, courageous men who will lead the world back to Christ. All of us should beg of God today a renewal of the grace of the sacrament of Confirmation that we may all be "radioactive" Catholics, soldiers of Christ, active members of Christ's army.

"Christ tells his apostles to be in the world for the
purpose of transfiguration. This means serving the world for
higher motives than mere self-interest, applause, and recognition.
This life of total dedication to the spiritual as well as material
welfare of one's neighbor, whether that is within the family circle, in
the neighborhood, in economic or political struggles, or on the
professional plane, can be sheer martyrdom. Christ served his
nation not by giving in to their materialistic messianic aspirations
but by showing them the true way to salvation,
the hard way."

The Modern Apostle by Louis J. Putz, CSC (1957) p. 133

Chapter 5
The Christian Family Movement

The Christian Family Movement (CFM) is often acclaimed as the most successful creation of specialized Catholic Action in the United States. Msgr. Donald Kanaly was one of the early Chaplains for the three movements: Young Christian Students, Young Christian Workers and the Christian Family Movement. The latter encapsulated many aspects of all of Catholic Action, and this makes it an excellent laboratory for the study of U.S. Catholic Action—and for Catholic Action's relevance for today.

(Author's note: A skilled researcher and writer named Jeffrey M. Burns has published an absorbing history of CFM titled *Disturbing the Peace*: *A History of the Christian Family Movement* [1949–1974, Notre Dame, Ind.: University of Notre Dame Press, 1999] that can serve as a platform for reflections and conclusions. Burns notes that many people have taken credit for CFM. Father Putz had brought the concept of Observe, Judge and Act, from The French Young Christian Workers (JOC), to the United States from Europe and was the first CFM chaplin in the Movement.)

The roots of the movement were on the Notre Dame campus, where a group of male students came together in 1940 under the aegis of Catholic Action to discuss the Bible's implications for their social responsibilities as students and future social leaders. However, the war claimed them, and after it they returned as married men. Relishing their earlier experience, they now wanted to include their wives. CFM formally came about apparently in the following way. On his 1946 trip to Prague, Fr. Putz stopped in France to renew his contacts with the JOC and learned that the top leadership was developing the Mouvement Populaire des Familles, or people's family movement. Because its membership consisted of an entirely lay crowd, the episcopacy was suspicious of it and never gave approval.

Told about this group, a South Bend couple named Burnie and Helene Bauer decided to start a similar organization. On St. Patrick's Day of 1947, the first meeting was held in the Bauer home, and it adopted the same procedure that the student YCS groups had used earlier. The small houses and the agenda dictated that no more than six couples could participate in any group. The idea caught on in the Vetville groups that Fr. Hesburgh chaplained as well as in several parishes.

Each meeting had three parts. Following a brief open prayer the first part was a discussion of a Scripture text after a short prayer. The passage had been selected to throw light on the Christian's social responsibility. The host couple would examine the text in advance with the help of a chaplain so as to prevent the discussion from degenerating into an interpretation of the text. Otherwise, the chaplain's role was passive; he must not take the lead from the lay couples. The couples found the discussion phase highly stimulating because it often threatened to run on too long, so a 20-minute limit was imposed with an additional benefit of frequently leaving the couples feeling the need to continue the discussion among themselves later, as they might not have done without this limit.

The second part, termed a liturgy, actually was a discussion of Church principles and doctrines in relation to the couples' responsibilities as spouses and parents. Subjects might include Baptism, Confirmation, Marriage, Sunday worship, the reality of the Church, religious practices in the home, or any of a thousand other topics. The host couple prepared the content in advance. Great care was taken that all the couples participate, and that the meeting not decline into a monologue or a sermon.

The third part turned from theory and theology to actions. Now the couples discussed how to transform the doctrine into action in the neighborhood, schools, economy, recreation, politics, or race relations. The same discussion could extend over six or more months. In this phase, the group applied the JOC Inquiry method: observe, judge and act. For example, if the problem was unfriendliness in the neighborhood, it would be thoroughly discussed to uncover the facts and causes. A judgment or decision followed about each couple's responsibility for bringing about an improvement. Next an action was adopted—for example, a hot-dog roast—that could involve the couples singly or together. The action might seem simple, but often had unexpected ramifications. The details of the action were worked out in the meeting's final phase: the social part. These were kept simple in order that they keep their focus on whatever the action required. All the couples had to agree ahead of time on the action in this last part which had to be simple.

In this procedure, the couples deepened and internalized their own faith, were reaffirmed in it by others, and developed it further through intimate and sustained contact with others with similar concerns and problems. Combining theory and practice, the meeting was a total encounter with life. It examined the whole world through the eyes of the family. It enriched family life and directed its energies toward creative directions. As the couples learned from each other, their perspectives widened. The group brought religion and concrete life together, enabling the couples to make the Gospels real. At the same time, the group supplied part of the community that urban society lacked. The effects on others influenced by the group was contagious.

At about the same time, an energetic Chicago lawyer named Patrick Crowley, influenced by Monsignor Hillenbrand's Catholic Action priests, convoked a group of men that met periodically in his office. Soon their wives began meeting separately in a Wilmette parish organization. The men's group heard about Putz and invited him to their meetings. At his first encounter with them, he suggested that they henceforth include their wives, as did the South Bend couples. This suggestion was adopted. The Christian Family Movement was born when the groups from Chicago, South Bend and Milwaukee met at

Childerly Farm at Wheeling, Illinois, and adopted a name and program. A Yellow Book came out with a Gospel commentary, a liturgical discussion (at Monsignor Reynold Hillenbrand's insistence) and an Inquiry about social issues in the secular world. Patrick and Patty Crowley were elected the president couple, and the Catholic archdiocese of Chicago donated and furnished a headquarters on Superior Street in the cathedral parish.

In South Bend, CFM grew explosively; it was as if couples had been specifically waiting for it. Older pastors regarded it with suspicion, preferring the more traditionalist Legion of Mary, but younger, more modern clergy favored CFM. The liturgies were open to new forms of expression and more participation; thus, CFM prepared its members for the reforms of Vatican II.

Burns briefly sketched CFM's sociological contours. CFM was overwhelmingly middle class, although it had lower-class contingents in Woonsocket, Rhode Island, and Cleveland. Ralph and Reggie Weissert, CFM members in South Bend, were quoted as saying that CFM wanted and tried to attract black and poor couples as members, but encountered huge cultural barriers. Burns describes CFM-ers as the first generation of American Catholics to rise out of the lower class with no intention of falling back. According to Burns, CFM-ers were educated and had always been middle class. The move to the suburbs aggravated a problem that had momentous implications for the Church: the disappearance of natural communities on which religious communities must build. So, the need to find a new way to express Catholic identity had intersecting natural and religious causes, and CFM tried to fill it on both levels. CFM-ers who insisted that CFM's role was to support the family thought this conflicted with CFM's social mission—and they were correct. The conflict became the cause of CFM's eventual demise when social conditions shifted yet again.

The CFM membership, mostly middle-class and seeking a way to express its Catholic identity in new social conditions, was already half-secularized: torn between its loyalty to American institutions and its loyalty to Catholic spirituality. This inner division was none of its fault. American Catholics could not have been expected to renounce the real and palpable benefits of American democracy and economics. Almost all sensed a conflict between the two traditions, yet that somehow they were congruent. The difference seemed to arise from the spiritual tradition's recommendation of poverty of spirit (even outright material poverty) and self-abasement. The American Catholic laity could not resolve the tension abstractly.

One contribution of the Catholic Church to American culture was its communal principle, but in fact, the principle was mostly dormant inside the Church.

What do we mean by community? There is a precise explanation. A real community is a group that meets two tests: 1) the members of the group put their lives into each other's hands; and 2) any member at any time can—and most members eventually will—become a leader. Any group that does not meet these criteria is a community only in a diluted way. The personal benefit of a real community is that it deepens and enriches the life of each member as nothing else can. In short, this means that the human personality is socially constituted. The social benefit is that the group becomes incomparably flexible and resourceful, able to meet problems much better than do abstract organizations, and to respond in more creative ways, by calling up the resources it most needs at any time.

Reggie Weissert takes exception to the claim that CFM was not sufficiently communal, and because she was present at the creation, her objection deserves close scrutiny. She expressed it by referring to a story that became a legend throughout American Catholic Action and in which she played an integral role.

The CFM cell of which she and her husband were members had two member couples each with a mentally retarded child living at home. The group talked about this issue for a while and prayerfully decided to adopt it as their project. It investigated what facilities were available and found none anywhere in Indiana. More shockingly, a survey turned up no fewer than 100 similar children in the city. The group went to certain Notre Dame professors for help and enlisted the aid of labor unions, business leaders and local newspapers, while conducting a series of forums. These efforts raised enough funds to rent an unused school building, hire specialists and start a school. Members of labor unions came in to refurbish the building for free—almost unheard of at that time. The group gathered support and went to the state legislature to promote new facilities throughout the state, and it succeeded. The facility that the group founded in South Bend still exists and thrives. This success became an electrifying example throughout the Catholic Action world.

Another example of how CFM was truly communal was the creation of a Spanish Center in Joliet, IL. CFM couples had been working with migrant worker families and directly experienced the abominable living conditions and exploitation at the farms around their city. Before long their presence led many farmers, recognizing the danger to the status quo, to refuse these new friends of the migrant workers—once at the business end of a shotgun—to enter their property.

Many other CFM groups from surrounding areas, having had similar experiences, arrived at the same conclusion, and a meeting was called to discuss their observations. It was attended by a Maryknoll priest, Fr. Tom Peyton, and his colleague. They had vast knowledge on the subject and had no need to further educate the assemblage. Their role was to encourage the already-convinced that being truly Christian meant following firm convictions to the extent that they became empowered by the knowledge and reality to undertake the steps called for by the situation.

It was obvious that a site was needed away from the many restrictive migrant-worker farms where help might be obtained. The immediate needs of food, clothing, and other basics could be distributed from a store front, garage, or any other facility enabling important interchange that could ultimately lead to more lasting solutions.

Providentially, a large old home located in a poor section of town came on the market. The price was low, as the well-worn place needed work, but it was near where the workers went to shop. Guided by the Holy Spirit, one of the couples assessed their finances and offered to take a second mortgage on their home (and that of six offspring as well) as a guarantee to the bank if a down payment could be raised. In addition to pledging money for a down payment, each couple pledged monthly donations to keep the center going. This caused the Bishop, who had previously told a delegation of CFMers that his advisor told him there were no problems among the Spanish speaking, to reconsider his decision and promise financial assistance from the diocese.

Thus the Spanish Center was born and went on—through food, clothing, English classes, driver's license training, and much more—to eventually become a rallying point for not only the migrant workers but the entire Spanish community as well. After a few years, they were able to hire a Spanish-speaking priest who, in addition to serving the spiritual needs of the community, old and newly arrived alike, was able to organize and, more important, guide the community to political awareness beyond anyone's original hopes.

The fact that it moved through two more locations and ultimately resulted in a free medical clinic, education center, sounding board, and location where the Spanish-speaking could come to be heard gave continuing evidence of strong community in the CFM family.

One member points to it as a sign that CFM was in fact communal, that the members did feel responsibility for each other and would help other families through crises, whether caused by death, finances or children. Into the project of a school for retarded children, for example, the couples sank much of their own money. They saw a need outside their own families and they met it.

Everyone who lives for any considerable period knows that one problem in life is that in taking action, group members must come to terms and understanding with other members with whom they are not always in agreement. Only a real community can overcome this formidable barrier, but once it does, it becomes incomparably creative and efficient.

The formation of a community was never a part of CFM's identity or mission. CFM couples committed themselves to meeting with other couples about every two weeks. At other times, they were atomized families within the dominant culture (which CFM often criticized). Each husband remained mainly an engineer, businessman, lawyer or teacher and secondarily a member of CFM, and every family was solely responsible for its own material support and could make no claim to help from other families (although it often may have been forthcoming nonetheless). CFM did not change the members' basic identities; it only added a new dimension of service, and CFM-ers remained otherwise indistinguishable from other Americans. There is no way to know if or how participation in CFM changed their view of their secular roles. Burns' book has no discussion of CFM's effects on the self-understandings among its own members. In Burns' book he shows that they acquired many life-long friends and an orientation toward service.

CFM peaked in 1964 with almost 50,000 member couples across the U.S. For the first 15 years of its explosive growth, CFM took varied paths. For the first year, couples followed what was called the "Yellow Book" due to the color of its cover. This was considered to be basic training in their attempts to observe situations, make judgments and arrive upon suitable actions to take in order to alleviate the perceived problem in light of the scripture passage selected for that particular meeting. These subjects were relatively simple and achieved their goal of couples becoming comfortable with this new technique.

In succeeding years, groups followed what was called a yearly inquiry book concerned with many varied subjects that were studied for one year at a time. These were as varied as integration, business ethics, school systems, politics (with many members running for elective positions within their communities) the economy, international life and many others. Sometimes it was deemed necessary to revisit a particular area in order to bring about the desired results.

A program committee consisting of not less than 6 nor more than 10 to 12 couples living in different parts of the U.S., Canada, and Mexico met at the beginning of each year to evaluate the effectiveness of the previous year's program and decide on subject matter for the year to come. They agreed on areas to be considered and took responsibility for sections with which they felt most capable. A glance at some of the books they used testifies to the professionalism and dedication with which they carried out their assignments. In those days—long before faxes and email—these couples would communicate progress, problem areas and new ideas with each other until they were satisfied with the materials. The couples in the movement came together for a yearly convention each summer and the program committee would set aside their own time to review and finalize the book for the coming year.

Many CFM couples used vacation time and brought their children to the conventions with them. The conventions were most often held on the Notre Dame campus. Present were large gatherings of children and the young adults in charge of baby sitting the children while their parents were in meetings and workshops. Often the couples brought YCS members from home with them as well as their own offspring who were of baby sitting age. Sports and other programs were planned for the youngsters being shepherded by males and females alike. Time would always be set aside for "Cola socials" for the sitters following the evening sessions. All of this was planned by another committee of couples. One can readily imagine the shudders on the part of the resident faculty, grounds keepers, housekeepers, and cafeteria workers as Fr. Ted Hesburgh enthusiastically welcomed the procession of heavily burdened station wagons approaching their beautiful campus. One ingenious father of a huge family of energetic progeny had converted an old school bus for their family's yearly trek from California to South Bend. Often couples would invite others from more distant homes to overnight stays as they processed to Notre Dame utilizing highways somewhat different from those today. Affluence wasn't much in evidence for those couples attempting to make ends meet while in the process of raising larger than average families. Impressing their fellow CFM-ers was not high on their list of priorities. The couple who could afford to fly their family was almost unheard of in those days.

Knowledgeable speakers from all over the globe—for example, Henri Nouwen, Martin Marty, Sr. Elizabeth McAllister, Bernard Cook, Sr. Corita Kent, Dan and Phil Berrigan, Ceasar Chavez and the Native American Activist Mike Chosa —plus others too numerous to mention, were welcomed to address the members who in turn eagerly welcomed such expertise. They would address the assembly on their particular field and workshops would follow. Months in advance, groups of couples would meet to decide which speakers to invite to address the convention in the various areas where they would be working that year.

Other couples assumed responsibility for planning the daily liturgies and for inviting clergy to celebrate them. They were also in charge of selecting the music to be used, finding musicians to perform them and coordinating rehearsals. As the movement became more international, these experiences were priceless to all who were able to participate.

There was also a large network of workers mainly from the Chicago office who were responsible for designing the cover, layout, editing and printing of each book while keeping the yellow book material updated.

Is it any wonder that CFM members have been known as genuinely passionate on the subject of the movement?

CFM sought personalism in its activities and programs. This is not entirely a criticism; the programs were arguably far better than anything else on the scene and Burns' descriptions of them are quite engaging.

CFM's leaders—Pat and Patty Crowley and Msgr. Hillenbrand—said that CFM's purpose was to form apostles, not to bring about major changes "in its own name." That was certainly true in a sense. Catholic Action never had and did not want an overall abstract program. Instead, its small groups were supposed to tease out unique solutions for local problems. That is what would make Catholic Action culturally creative. But the CFM statement sets up an opposition between apostles and major change, thereby suggesting Hillenbrand did not know what "real" Catholic Action was. Catholic Action emphatically did aspire to major change; its distinction was the route it chose to take. Another sign that Hillenbrand somehow missed the boat was the controlling role he seized in CFM and that his priests acquired in other Catholic Action activities in Chicago. They had to appease the liberal Cardinal Stritch. However, it would have been helpful if Hillenbrand could have noticed the anomaly.

Msgr. Hillenbrand was very insistent on always keeping the Movement properly focused as a Catholic Action movement. This was certainly not to be construed as a controlling role nor as an appeasement to Cardinal Stritch. CFM's thrust was, through group action, to gradually transform the secular world around it to a more Christian milieu.

CFM's areas of concentration were extensive: Politics, International Life, Liturgy, Economic Life, Family Life, Race, and Ecumenism among others. This larger exposure to the areas of their lives was intended to make lay people more conscious of the various areas of lay life to be Christianized and to form their minds for this task.

It should be noted that the CFM meetings and training so efficiently pre-dispositioned members' agreement with Vatican II that attempts to implement the documents took the time formerly spent on meetings, observations and actions. It was a rare pastor who whole-heartedly welcomed such things as responsible parish councils, liturgy committees, religious education directors (much less female ones!) and financial accountability to his congregation. In its efforts at assuming responsibility in areas for which they had already trained themselves, CFM members became too overworked to even consider beginning new "Yellow Book Groups." The notions of many members and chaplains concerning ecumenism further drove membership apart. Around this same time, CFM members became somewhat divided between those who felt they needed to center their energies on their families and those who favored pursuit of Catholic Action's social objectives. Their original purpose information—to develop ways to positively influence factors affecting family life—was being diverted by economic and environmental issues.

If Catholic Action was to address social institutions in the secularizing United States, the members had to find footing in a real community that would give them strength to oppose the secularist culture within their own selves. Why were individualism, materialism and secularism objectionable? How does one go about separating the good from the bad? Whatever the alleged Catholic "answer" was, it had something to do with community. Catholic people had to unlock and unleash it, and not simply by accident.

Hillenbrand's position at the center was undeniably positive in spite of his not seeing Catholic Action as did Putz, as a wedge for a better way of organizing the Church itself. A CFM community would have made Hillenbrand's position both untenable and unnecessary; CFM could not have allowed an outside figure such control over its material fortunes. The Inquiry method had CFM-ers pursue solutions for social problems in a way that was communal and non-individualist at its core. However, it could not help them in their own lives.

Burns' book is a description of CFM's considerable achievements and a chronicle of intense conflicts that sapped CFM's time eventually causing downsizing in numbers and brought it down.

The first conflict was that between Burnie Bauer and the Crowleys. Bauer, one of the original U.S. Catholic Actionists, seems to have viewed himself, reasonably, as CFM's real founder. He favored continuing actions that cumulatively could change local institutions to help local families, while the Crowleys favored educational and social awareness programs that would give families a better understanding of other people's needs. The Crowleys' vision tracked more closely the agenda of secular liberals, who, as rationalists, like to believe that the evils of the world are problems of cognition: spread around enough knowledge and understanding and they will be solved. The Church says the main problem is volitional: people either don't want the good or value lesser goods over greater. This is called sin. Although Putz once said (as a publisher) that his greatest regret with respect to CFM was that it couldn't interest its people enough in good reading, he didn't think it was an educational enterprise. Its purpose was action.

Besides Hillenbrand, the other force that held CFM together was Cardijn's Inquiry method. Burns treats it as mainly an organizing method, but it went much deeper. It expressed a spirituality in which Christian formation could occur only in and through action, as two facets of the same thing. There was a lasting conflict over whether CFM should focus on the family (internal community) or on social action (external community) and when social conditions shifted yet again the membership determined choices of focus would best be left to individual groups.

The average CFM couple remained in the organization only about three and a half years. Since a considerable number of couples stayed for almost fifty years, it seems that the median and more typical tenure was little more than three years. Because many of the changes resulting from Vatican II required lay leaders, many CFM couples volunteered to lead in the parish reform. CFM in one sense was the loser of many good leaders. In another sense, the local church was the beneficiary of their talents. Many moved on to equally fruitful lives as politicians or leaders of secular reform. But they could not hope to accomplish anything of what CA (and CFM as part of it) set out to do. Were they committed to CA's goals? Reading between the lines, one surmises that in many families secular overtook religious concerns. Or perhaps they suspected that CFM goals would not be accomplished within the church as it existed.

A second great conflict divided CFM almost from the start, between those who thought CFM's mission was to form and support families and those, including Bauer, Hillenbrand and the Crowleys, who said it must aim at social action. After about twenty years, the first group won (even Putz would admit this). A conflict over this should not have been possible, but both factions were correct: Hillenbrand and the Crowleys' view that social change was CFM's goal was valid; the familists' position also held true insofar as that if CFM could not achieve consensus within its own ranks, it could not promote it in society—the basic social change a Catholic reform movement had to pursue. The insistence on family was a disguised call for deeper community, and many of the objections Burns quotes members as raising seem to have that thrust. The families were not getting the support they needed to do the work CFM took on. This may have caused as many to move on as correction of it might have caused to stay and to thrive. Turnover might have slowed even more than perhaps recruitment. In the 1960s' pseudo-communal counter-culture, CFM might even have become trendy and relevant, rather than just one more tired outlet for lay activism. As it was, CFM became polarized along as many vectors as the secular culture itself.

While arguably a quite well-written account, one of the few problems in Burns' history is that he needed an overall framework or theme to give the story coherence. He reached for the image of an avant garde, a secular concept based on the myth of Progress. To be avant garde, CFM must always be at the leading edge on all issues, religious or secular. CFM was certainly more advanced, especially in the eyes of hierarchy. However, CFM was far from progressive in secular terms. Its basic goal—to bring secular structures more into line with the requirements of Catholic life and faith—was reactionary to secularists. So, Burns oscillates between a secularist and religious appreciation of CFM: secularist when measuring CFM against the Church institution, and religious and Catholic when measuring it against secular society. He brags that CFM promoted in advance the Second Vatican Council's endorsement of lay involvement, even though after the council, CFM-ers turned away from involvement with the world for greater involvement inside the Church. Late in the 1960s, a national chaplain said CFM lay persons should think more about the welfare of the community, and many CFM-ers thought he wanted to deter them from involvement in the Church. Burns writes that as progressive as the council's documents were, they still had not caught up to CFM. Perhaps this is the case, but of which CFM focus do we speak? Is it the focus envisioned by Catholic Action or the one almost forced by its inner tensions to become secular? He says that Pat and Patty Crowley's position on birth control was, in contrast to Pope Paul VI's, simple common sense. In short, one could possibly regard CFM as both reactionary and radical.

Burns also pays little attention to the shift in the secular culture that affected life inside the Church as strongly as life outside it. The secular shift overwhelmed the Church reform started by Vatican II. Those in the Church receptive to change pulled back from it as un-Catholic or secular, others became radicalized, and the application of divine truth became uncertain except on the most basic level. One principle had endured (inside the Church): the person of Jesus Christ and His absolute centrality for each person and for the community that belief in Him creates.

Burns notes that in the 1970s, some Catholics tired of social questions and turned inward, participating in such movements as Cursillo and Marriage Encounter and trying to work out laboriously for themselves how to live a Christian life in the new social dispensation. But that was a retreat from engagement, and not, as he implies, just a neutral cultural phase. Again, a thriving CFM was sorely missed.

The lasting conflict over whether CFM should focus on the family (internal community) or on social action (external community) intensified. The leadership's insistence on social action was correct and essential from Catholic Action's point of view, but their program had a secular flavor, in fact was almost the same as that of secular liberals. There may actually be nothing objectionable about it to some, but others might say that perhaps CFM should have come up with its own solutions. The secret reason why secular reform is impersonal and programmatic is the difficulty of interpersonal engagement, a reality far easier to ignore or dismiss than to solve.

If there was a single underlying deficiency in CFM, it was the lack of trained and committed priests, chaplains in the Movement. Putz, Hillenbrand and a few others got together but active CFM chaplains were too few to continue to form the lay people. More of them were needed to enlarge and make more effective lay apostles on a long term basis.

Also, too few of the hierarchy were involved. Members may well have spent more time battling them, which discouraged a lot of lay people from actual commitment. Unfortunately, many of them did not support the teachings and direction of Vatican II.

A newer cause of conflict within CFM was the ecumenist thrust pushed by some who thought that combining with other denominations could increase CFM's impact and generate more realistic solutions. The liturgy committee invited the Episcopal priest (the priest and his wife had long been members of the CFM Program Committee that wrote the inquiry book) to celebrate a Mass at the national convention. When some of the Catholic hierarchy learned of this, a huge uproar ensued and CFM lost the (Catholic) bishops for good. Burns applies the avant garde label to this, as if the ecumenists could brush aside the doctrinal differences as irrelevant, or the definition of what solutions were realistic would not depend on what denomination was doing the defining. (Author's note: when the abortion controversy later erupted, CFM found itself on the other side from many of the denominations it had invited to participate.) Mere doctrinal questions were at the root of the Church's problems with the modern world and, as Burns wrote, the move to become an interfaith organization signaled the creation of a radically different identity for CFM. Hillenbrand, who believed that correct liturgical form was almost more important than social action, was permanently embittered.

By that time, few issues were being examined more than superficially. In the mid-sixties, Larry Ragan, the gifted editor of CFM's newsletter, ACT, threw his pages open for unrestricted debate. (Author's note: he later founded a publishing empire aimed at corporate communications utilizing CFM newsletters as well as annual conferences.) Although free debate is necessary in democratic society, and perhaps even in the Church, not so in Catholic Action, where the legitimate subject for discussion was how to accomplish CFM's objective, not CFM's reason for existing, much less the nature of the Church. Opening ACT's columns to free debate helped to convert CFM from action to polemics. When argument became chic and usurped CFM's official goals, CFM was already as good as finished.

More a symptom than a cause of CFM's problems, the ecumenism push was another sign that CFM was losing its focus. With its ear to the ground, Fides Press had detected the two key changes in the religious situation in the 1960s: a blurring of denominational lines and a greater emphasis on the human and less on institutionalized religion, now seen as having no contact with real life in the Secular City. So CFM's ecumenical push was in style; the danger was that the style might change again just as abruptly. In addition, civil rights was one of the few issues on which most Christians were on the same page, and the euphoria that capped the crusade's public success prompted the avant garde to try, prophetically, to push ecumenical cooperation in new areas where it could bury problems in good will. CFM thus could recapture the success it had enjoyed in the 1950s. But the list of real possibilities was short. Would Lutherans and Episcopalians support federal funding for parochial schools, an urgent question for the Catholic parents in CFM? It is difficult to think of a benefit that the CFM organization or the public would have derived from going ecumenical. Almost all of CFM's work was at the grass roots, where it should have been easy for CFM groups to join with other denominations interested in similar projects. The advantage of bringing them into CFM is not obvious—unlike the disadvantage. Could a minister be substituted for a priest without loss of anything essential, in a CFM whose action/formation process was saturated with Catholic values and understandings? But as Burns points out, the priest was now irrelevant in CFM. In the late 1960s, many Catholics abandoned belief in the "real presence," Heaven and Hell, and sacramental confession, so the avant garde may not have been an unmitigated blessing for the Church.

There were other conflicts over a secular vs. a religious consciousness, between the center (organization) and the "grass roots" (community), between experienced and newer couple members, between witness and conversion, liberals and conservatives, laity and clergy, and over birth control and race. The number and intensity of conflicts may be measures of CFM's diversity and vitality.

It seems that CFM—lay-based, concerned with the family, and a rich source of practical information on sexuality—could have helped the Church adjust to the post-Vatican II era. But its leadership, resolving to champion issues of justice in the secular world, discovered to its surprise that much of its constituency were conservatives who thrived under CFM's emphasis on the family and deplored the ecumenical tack promoted by the liberals. But as the lay people best prepared to implement the Council's directives, the liberals soon were drawn off from CFM by other Church matters. When Pat and Patty Crowley served on the Vatican-appointed lay commission that recommended relaxation of the prohibition on birth control, CFM's fate was sealed. Tainted, in the minds of some, by leftist ideology, it disintegrated. It struggled on, a mere shadow, and still exists today, focusing on personal sanctity and family improvement rather than specifically outreach.

For Catholic Action, including CFM, there was one basic issue: the culture was revolving around an economics organized and monopolized by rationalists. Nothing much could be done about other issues until this one was addressed, except to move the pieces around on the board.

CFM brought something unique and priceless to cultural and social action: its personalist orientation and perspective. One summer CFM convention participants were treated to the presence and performances of Ray Repp (then all the rage) and Cyril Paul of Lord of the Dance fame during various liturgies and social events. These dramatically culminated at Sunday morning liturgy by the presence of the now deceased Father Clarence Rivers leading his mass dedicated to the brotherhood of all mankind accompanied by the South Bend Symphony Orchestra and a huge well rehearsed chorus. Thus the families' return trips home were full of song in their hearts, minds and voices.

"In recent years the Popes have stressed the doctrine
of the Mystical Body and the necessity of the lay apostolate.
There is an intimate connection between the two.
While Catholics in general have developed a deep faith
in the sacramental presence of Christ and profound appreciation
for the role played by the priest, there is a considerable
lag in the awareness of the Church
as the People of God."

The Modern Apostle by Louis J. Putz, CSC (1957) p. 20

Shown above is South Bend, Indiana, resident Reggie Weissert. She was a close friend of Father Putz. This memorial bench is outside of the office of Chuck Lennon, Executive Director of the Notre Dame Alumni Association at Notre Dame.

The members of the original board of the Notre Dame Senior Service Team donated funds for the bench in thankful memory for the founding inspiration of Father Louis.

A tradition was formed to hold Father Putz style of action oriented prayer sessions. This is held at the bench on every occasion the board meets on the Notre Dame campus.

Many friends of Father Putz stop at the bench for a moment of pause, reflection and prayer.

Chapter 6

Seminary Reformer

In 1963, a man walked into Louis Putz's office at Fides Press on Bulla Road and introduced himself as James Michael Lee, a professor of education at Notre Dame. He told Putz that he had long had a strong interest in Catholic religious education and believed that the main problem in Catholic schools originated in seminaries. According to Lee, priests used their clerical authority to interfere in elementary schools but knew little about education. Lee proposed that Fides publish a book that would expose the defects in the education that went on in seminaries themselves.

Lee was something of a maverick himself. After earning a Master's degree in History at Columbia University, he had added a doctorate in education from Columbia's Teacher's College, and then taught at a small college in Connecticut. He then wrote a book on Catholic secondary education that McGraw-Hill published, and the book won him an invitation to join the Education Department at Notre Dame. At first he aimed his next book, on seminary education, at improving Catholic schooling, but gradually broadened its scope in his own mind to benefiting the entire Church.

But Lee faced a serious problem. The Church as a whole, including even progressive theologians such as Yves Congar, regarded religious education—not to mention education in seminaries—as a strictly clerical preserve. Lee needed some sort of cover or front to address the matter.

When Lee proposed that Fides do a book on seminary education, Putz became greatly excited and almost immediately agreed. Lee told him the book should be both innovative and deeply scholarly. He listed a series of famous authors whom he hoped to attract as contributors. Again, Putz agreed. The next question was who would edit the book, which would be a series of essays dealing with every aspect of seminary education. Putz said that of course Lee must do it. However, Lee replied that if a lay person were the editor, the hierarchy would never take the book seriously. The editor should be a cleric. They soon reached agreement that they would co-edit the book and that Lee's name would go first, for that was crucial for Putz's own apostolate and for that of Fides on behalf of the laity.

The resulting book, *Seminary Education in a Time of Change*, was probably the most influential book Fides ever published and it spread Putz's name and reputation more widely in the Church than did all his previous work. Put on a fast track within Fides, the book was published at a most opportune moment: March 1965, as the famous council was drawing to a close and expectations were high for dramatic changes, especially among the clergy. The book exploded like an atomic bomb in the sheltered world of seminaries. Fortunately, Putz had provided cover by persuading the "moderate" Cardinal Ritter of St. Louis to write the foreword. Actually, Lee wrote the foreword and signed the cardinal's name to it. Therefore, the book came out with a sort of official approval that seminary rectors could not ignore.

The reaction among seminary rectors was furious, but through a Fides publicist, Putz was able to get the two editors a spot as featured speakers at the prestigious summer National Catholic Education Convention in New York's Hilton Hotel. The special meeting for the rectors in the Seminary Division was scheduled for a Wednesday evening, when normally most delegates would be out on the town. But when Lee and Putz entered the room, it was crowded with rectors, standing two or three deep around the walls.

Lee said the crowd was really a lynch mob, but its target was Lee and not Putz. Lee was puzzled that Putz let him take almost all the heat. Lee found himself holding off the attack almost alone, but remained composed and responded as best he could with logic. He speculates that he was the target because he was a layman and his name had appeared first on the title page, while Putz was a priest and also held his tongue. Lee was hurt, even in his later years, by Putz's failure to rise to his defense, but the obvious explanation is that Lee could afford to take the heat while Putz could not, because he had already expended all of his political capital in earlier wars. *Newsweek* magazine devoted a whole page to the showdown.

The rectors had four main objections to the book. They protested that the book saw the seminary more as a place for education than for formation. They objected to the description of priesthood as a profession rather than a vocation. They also objected to the contentions that "minor" (high school) seminaries should be closed and that most major seminaries were too small to provide quality education and should be consolidated.

The book is widely credited with ushering in and deciding the direction of seminary reform both in the U.S. and throughout the world. Although its proposals were strongly resented and opposed at first, within five years they had all become standard in most seminaries. The Church now takes all this for granted, but it is arguable that Putz, Lee and the book saved the Church from far worse turmoil than it actually experienced during the next thirty years. It provided a roadmap to guide and structure an upheaval that already had become inevitable. Had Lee not been nursing his ideas and this project as early as 1956, and Putz not been available to publish them, events could have turned out far worse than they did.

Additionally, it turned out that Putz would not only provide an abstract description of what a reformed seminary should be, but also an actual, living, breathing model that all other seminaries could key on.

Early in the 1960s, when Vince Giese left Fides to become a priest, Putz petitioned his superiors for release from his teaching duties at Notre Dame so as to undertake more important full-time work at Fides. They agreed, but a short time later he was serving for a few months, reportedly on a sabbatical, as the chaplain in a convent in Princeton, New Jersey. When he returned to Notre Dame, he installed himself for a year in the campus firehouse as chaplain. A close C.S.C. associate of later years says Putz was in the administration's doghouse because he was considered a "loose cannon," but others say the firehouse gave him more freedom. That seems more likely. He went on a fire run with his helmet on backwards, and the consummately professional fire chief, a C.S.C. brother, asked him to forgo more trips.

Putz was never popular within his own congregation, partly because he was not an intellectual, and the congregation had a heavy commitment to education. He worked mainly with laity rather than clergy, and he did not defer to power nor cultivate those who had it—and they resented him for that. But the main objection to him was that he had found a new way of living a clerical life, a freer way than had the others who were in a traditional "straitjacket" (resentment against which exploded in the 1960s). The fact that laity sensed this difference in him probably accounts for the adulation and affection they heaped on him; and that appeal further reduced his charm for other members of his particular religious order. Generally an organization will push such people aside until it really needs them in a crisis that the traditional system cannot handle. It then turns reluctantly to the non-conformist for help, but only until the situation can be re-stabilized.

Fortunately for Putz, the congregation's problems were becoming greater than his. It was beginning to experience difficulty in attracting and retaining new members. This was a long-term death sentence for the order. Fr. Howard Kenna was in charge and saw Putz as a solution—very probably the only solution. The great success of Putz's book on seminary education had suggested that he might have some answers. In one chapter, Putz had argued that seminaries must be reorganized around their crucial mission to prepare for and support the laity's mission to the world, on which, according to Putz, the Church's future depended.

He also had authored a short article, "A Plea for New Seminary Structures," that attempted a psychological and spiritual profile of a new breed of applicants to seminaries. It transposed onto seminary students the standard depiction of the baby boom generation, with a few small variations for spirituality. Putz cited no sources in the article but its terms and concepts were unusual for him, so it is unlikely that he came up with the ideas on his own. The article described the new seminarian as a product of a home with a traditional respect for normal means of salvation—sacraments, Masses, rosaries, Benediction, and the Blessed Sacrament—that had lost resonance in the lives of students, who were unwilling to accept older realities on simple faith. The new generation was said to be highly critical, concerned about self-development and freedom, anti-institutional and anti-structuralist, dedicated to experimentation, wary of dichotomies such as natural-supernatural, sacred-profane, and church-state, and wholly focused on the future while disdainful of the past. Thus the authoritarian system in the seminary was passé on sociological grounds, irrespective of theology. Needed was a horizontal system of formation in place of the vertical and authoritarian, and more personal interaction in place of mere structure—in short, a whole new structure of values.

Putz offered this profile in a sociological mode without commenting on its deeper value issues. Later events showed that the young were less alienated from the system than they had pretended. In the 1990s, those who had been young in the sixties favored a market economy. It seemed that the new morality was contingent on continuation of the painless 1960s prosperity.

It is impossible to know, but perhaps easy to guess, what went through Louis Putz's mind when his friend Fr. Kenna made a startling proposition!

Howard Kenna was an unusual man and priest—a solid and unassuming administrator with a perceptive and canny mind. He had earlier occupied positions in his order as academic vice president at Notre Dame, as the second man in charge of the entire congregation, and as president of The University of Portland, Oregon. To nominate a slightly suspect radical activist like Putz to be head of the order's seminary took insight and courage. But Kenna had known and liked Putz since their early days in minor seminary had bestowed an honorary doctorate on him at Portland. He knew that the unusually deep crisis required a visionary response. For Putz, the nomination was a welcome institutional validation of his work, giving him new status in his community. Yet, it was a gamble for Kenna and presented Putz with a difficult choice.

Putz possessed the creative qualities of a good publisher and he also had proven himself to be a born organizer. An organizer must envision a new possibility clearly, believe in it, and be able to inspire in others the confidence to reach for and achieve it. Yet he also must be a realist, able to distinguish the difficult from what is truly impossible.

When the call from Kenna came, Putz must have known that to accept meant to abandon the work into which he had poured 30 years of his life. True, he would be addressing an important aspect of the laity-in-the-Church issue. And when he went to the seminary he retained many of his responsibilities at Fides as well as his older associations. His causes might flounder if he surrendered them. A sixth sense told him the moment for Catholic Action was passing, that the tide had shifted and was moving, as yet ever so slowly, in a new direction. Fr. Chester Soleta, a long-time and astute academic vice-president at Notre Dame, said that what he admired most about Louis Putz was his ability to walk away from a major project or even a life's work and start something new. Putz accepted the challenge to refashion the seminary, and to do that he had to drop YCS.

Years later, he offered a rationale. In its early days, YCS and CFM were charting virgin territory against strong resistance even from priests and nuns, who mainly controlled the Church landscape. Notre Dame's own President, John O'Hara, saw Catholic Action as communistic yet rose to high office in the Church. Other lay organizations, such as Holy Name societies, served mainly the Church and had little interest in anything outside it. However, he said that Vatican II generalized the concept embodied by Catholic Action. (This enabled Putz, in his own writings, to shift from use of the more vague Mystical Body imagery, legitimated by Pius XII in an encyclical as a justification for Catholic

Action, to Congar's People of God imagery, which was suspect until the Council adopted it.) What propelled American Catholics out of their "ghetto" may not have been the election of John F. Kennedy but that of John XXIII as Pope, who in a short year or two swept away the prejudices of centuries. As Catholics acquired full membership in secular society, the "specialized apostolates" of YCS, YCW, and CFM lost their cachét and their recruits to broader, more secular alternatives such as the Peace Corps, the Civil Rights movement, the War on Poverty, and even the Papal Volunteers, while the few priests available to Catholic Action declined sharply as priests shucked the cloth in droves. When a laity that had seen themselves as American Catholics began to view itself instead as Catholic Americans, Catholic Action appeared to be doomed.

Putz's showdown with the seminary system had been long incubating. Few people could have had a more negative experience with it than his and survived. The extreme austerity and isolation might have been nourishing or tolerable to a more "spiritual" or intellectual soul, but to the gregarious and relationship-oriented Putz it had been a severe trial. Even his seminary experience in France had presented a dramatic contrast to it and suggested some features that should characterize a thorough reform. His goal was simple: to reorient the seminary system away from the intense interiority that had once prepared priests for their conservative clerical role in a static society and toward engagement with the dynamic lay world with which the future of the Church clearly lay.

As ever, the Church's main mission was to evangelize the world, and that responsibility now rested largely with the laity. But they could not do it except as fully functioning and integrated members of the Church society. To assume a leadership role in evangelizing, they first must develop their leadership abilities inside the Church. At stake in the question of the laity's role in the Church is the Church's role in the world. The laity must at least be consulted in the work of evangelization, not simply issued orders.

It was precisely in his role and experience as a maverick that Putz now became indispensable to the universal Church. A better encultured priest would have felt compelled to proceed cautiously and carefully. Putz knew that a piecemeal reform would be a disaster, crippling hopes and allowing resistance to solidify. Instead, the entire system must be changed overnight, coming like a bolt out of the blue. As he admitted (discounting his earlier slight responsibilities in France), he had virtually no experience with seminaries. All he had to work with for an organizational model was his work in Catholic Action, so in effect, he began to apply it here. His first step was to announce that by the next day the seminarians must have prepared a written constitution for the seminary. Students were shocked and set adrift. Some never fully adapted.

One of his first needs was to install a staff congenial to him and his program, and he had personal magnetism enough to attract priests of the highest quality, including the brilliant Chester A. Soleta, John S. Dunne, William Lewers (future superior of the province), the great John Egan of YCW fame in Chicago, Henri Nouwen, and several more. The ability to attract to his projects such able people marked him conspicuously throughout his life.

Putz's decisiveness reminds us of Harry Truman. Both are examples that a seemingly ordinary person may be more capable of carrying the mantle of leadership than the best and brightest who went to the finest schools and entered early into positions of responsibility and authority. Like Truman, Putz did not possess eloquence, good looks, or charm, and, although very bright, was neither accused of being an intellectual nor of having political presence. Truman was known to his friends simply as Harry; Putz was known as Louie. Both were born poor and worked into their later years on farms. Putz was denied permission to attend Harvard, Truman never went to college. Truman joined the National Guard in order to participate in the great national effort in World War I. The turning point in his life occurred on almost the same fields as did Putz's, and only a few years earlier. Truman's fellow guardsmen on the front sensed something unusual in him and elected him their first lieutenant, although he had no connections of any kind. He was put in charge of Battery D of the 2nd battalion of the 129th Field Artillery, Dizzy D as it was called; a notoriously rowdy group of about 200 soldiers. The men gave Harry hell on his first day in command. They stampeded their horses. They brawled in the barracks. They gave him a Bronx cheer. Truman later recalled that the task of taking command was more frightening than heavy combat.

Nevertheless, he acted swiftly and decisively. The following morning he publicly busted several non-commissioned officers, beginning with the First Sergeant. Then he called the other non-commissioned officers into his tent and told them: "I didn't come over here to get along with you. You've got to get along with me. And if there are any of you who can't, speak up right now and I'll bust you back too." After that, Truman remembered, "we got along." Truman turned one of the worst batteries in the regiment into one of the best. "You soldier for me," he told his men, "and I'll soldier for you."

How did Truman intuitively grasp one of the cardinal principles of leadership: the importance, in a new situation, of not wasting any time in demonstrating determination to lead in a certain way and a certain direction? This is also the mystery of Louis Putz.

A first principle for Putz was that seminary students should receive an education resembling, as closely as possible, that of other students. The healthy competition and the wholesome contact with those the seminarian would eventually serve as a priest was crucial. The seminary should be located near a university and the seminarians should dress like other students.

Formerly, seminarians had lived in large buildings organized by rules and regulations, but were much alone and interacted little. Putz thought that living in community required the formation of small teams of six to ten members who interacted closely with each other, took charge of their own lives, and as much as possible made their own decisions. No other way could break down the old style of regimentation and conformity. The team was a living community with strong personal communication. Each was assigned a chaplain or moderator playing much the same role that a chaplain performed in Catholic Action. Tasks that had belonged to the superior and his assistants devolved now to the teams, which elected members to seminary-wide committees to form policies on everything from recreation to sports to curricula. Seminarians sensitive to liturgies could take initiative in designing them. One night each week, the committees reported their recommendations to the entire student body and submitted them to a vote. Thus seminarians became accustomed to democratic methods. The team helped the individual to relate at once to God and to others, while the committees enabled the whole community to function in a way most acceptable to all. Each student could express himself in the full assembly every week.

An especially important committee was the apostolic committee. This group concerned itself with the seminarians' involvement with lay groups during the year and in the summers, commitments in which seminarians learned to make judgments and decisions. Some worked on racial justice, some with migrant laborers; others went to the inner city, and still others to schools. Putz saw involvement in apostolic work as the only way a seminarian could learn to become apostolic. Involvement in lay-oriented work would teach the future priest respect for the laity's competence. And Putz believed that laity had a right to participate in the training of those who would be their ministers.

The daily and weekly schedules were reduced to a bare minimum, and imposed asceticism was largely eliminated in favor of the student's ability to make his own sacrifices. The teams, and the individuals in them, organized their own time. Collectively, there was only general Morning Prayer, an informal buffet lunch, and vespers and Mass before supper. Saturdays were almost entirely unscheduled. By all accounts there was no advocacy or support of advanced understandings on sexual and other moral matters. Putz remained a strict traditionalist in his piety and cultural positions, and liberal only in organizational matters, especially whatever concerned the laity's position in the institutional Church.

Almost any feature of the new system could have jumped up to bite him, so to speak. The one that actually did so was, surprisingly, the Sunday liturgy (formerly, a Mass). Like other aspects of the seminary, this was redesigned to be open to the world, with revitalized music and some of the country's best preachers, including Notre Dame's own John S. Dunne and Henri Nouwen. The liturgy was opened to outsiders, who flocked to it in droves, first from the campus, soon from the surrounding areas. Eventually, the local pastors began to miss some of their best parishioners and their contributions and bombarded the local bishop, Leo Pursley, with assertions about heresy on the march at Moreau. Putz had offered them a target by inviting suspect people, such as the Berrigan brothers, the two theologian Bernards, Cook and Haering, Susan B. Anthony (the great reformer's niece), and others, to speak at the seminary. The bishop vociferated a threat of suspension for Putz and interdict for the seminary.

But Putz had experience with opposition. Sweetly, he invited Pursley to the seminary to see for himself. Pursley was taken aback, but being a fair man, rose to the bait. He refused to set foot in the seminary but agreed to a showdown with Putz at the order's provincial headquarters. To this fateful meeting Putz took an array of well-prepared counselors, and the bishop came fortified with his own (whom, Putz said later, sympathized more with his position than with the bishop's). Pursley's men laid out their objections, which the Notre Dame theologians easily but respectfully knocked down. By the end of the meeting Pursley backed off, without losing his concern for his local pastors. The meeting ended in a restrained cordiality and, although the diocese never sent any of its recruits to the seminary, Pursley welcomed Putz into one of the diocese's own departments after he withdrew from his position in the seminary. No heresy charges came to light. Putz did not see critics as enemies. He claimed that he had good relations with Pursley from that day on.

This encounter between the reformer and the bishop was as paradigmatic as anything else about the seminary reform. As Fr. Putz later confessed, although his reform swelled the ranks of candidates, it did not appreciably slow the rate of defections. For its thrust blurred the distinction between the clergy and the laity, by seeming to laicize the clergy just as Vatican II was clericalizing lay people by opening multitudinous new ministries to them. One result was an eclipse of the long Catholic tradition that the priest is another Christ. If the priest's main role is simply to empower others, what is the point of celibacy or ordination? If asked, Louis Putz probably would have said that there is no question that the priest is another Christ. However, so is any baptized Catholic; and sorting out the difference is not easy. However, Pursley had a point, and his willingness (rather unusual among bishops, as it later turned out) to confront the reformer makes him equally a hero in the story. If the reform obscured the intrinsic dignity of the priesthood, that was a shame. But as has been said, reforms by their nature grope existing methods and ideas while proposing new ones, and can find a new pattern only through trial and error.

Change in the Catholic Church for a long time had been almost impossible, because any proposal was denounced as a victory for Protestantism, secularism or heresy. Even reform in the Middle Ages had not faced that obstacle; it threatened material interests mainly (and these but marginally, because it took shape in mendicant orders devoted to poverty). In the embattled late-modern Church, pressures had to become explosive before even a slight change could occur. Even if it had failed, Putz's change in the seminary system might have performed a service by giving the Church empirical evidence of the effects of actual change. His new system appeared soon to have succeeded, or at least had not failed: Kenna said that it went more smoothly and created fewer problems than he had expected.

Yet management even of a reformed seminary constantly presented Putz with responsibilities, especially program and strategic planning, for which he was ill equipped by temperament. He expressed a desire to shuffle these burdens off, and only partly succeeded, and all this undoubtedly fueled some of the resistance he met. To some the new freedoms were welcome, to others they were chaotic. The maneuvering on which others might have thrived drained Putz's energy at a time when he was experiencing an alarmingly growing problem with arthritis. Some associates say he believed he could function henceforth only as a caretaker of a revolution already accomplished, and that he rejected such a passive role that would have ushered him into retirement when he wanted to resume his earlier life of action. In any case, when, after six tumultuous years, Kenna invited him to continue for another term, he declined, declaring that six years were enough for any superior and that his office needed new blood.

Putz later referred repeatedly to his distaste for the hassles he experienced as rector of a seminary. One of his favorite examples (probably because it made a good story) was his encounter with a seminarian named Edward "Monk" Malloy, the future President of Notre Dame. Malloy was a high-school teammate of John Thompson, a future famous coach at Georgetown, on a winning basketball team in Baltimore, and he was said to wield a quick and accurate long shot. Malloy had taken to organizing marathon late-night basketball games in the seminary gym, and after them he would invite the players to the kitchen for sandwiches he prepared. This habit put a huge dent in the seminary's food budget, and Putz felt obliged to confront Malloy about it. But in the meeting Malloy cheerfully offered to resign from the seminary. In its new concern for self-fulfillment, the new generation was perpetually testing (i.e., ambivalent about) its vocation and ready to reconsider at the smallest provocation. Entitled, it was also disinclined to pay the bills. In short, Putz repeatedly ran into a dark side of the "new freedom." His system was as much demanding of the rector as it was easier on the student, for the smallest matters now must be negotiated, sometimes endlessly, and (because of the students' immaturity) could balloon into major symbolic confrontations. That probably was not something Fr. Putz had anticipated.

Putz wanted to prepare seminarians to work as associates and support lay leaders. But many of the students doubted they would ever work in such a role or under such a system, and the next 30 years proved them to be correct. The whole point of the reform was that priests would support laity in their evangelization of the world. But evangelization didn't turn out to be popular among lay Catholics. Whatever the essential merits of Putz's new seminary, the ecclesial system it took for granted was one that neither the church hierarchy nor even the advanced elements of the laity had so much as faintly endorsed. Because of that, there was a conflict built into the new model, and many of the students sensed it. Putz could not reform the Church through the seminary, and when his imitators later tried to do exactly that, the reform went off the rails as progressives conducted their own long march through Church institutions. Putz had little interest in the internal cultural issues that agitated them.

A retrospective evaluation of Putz's early leadership of seminary reform must contend with these later developments that never affected him. Most important was post-modernism—i.e., secular rationalism's abandonment of the Enlightenment's faith in an impersonal and objective reason. Although in part healthy, in its secularist context this disillusionment presented formidable new dangers, especially its conclusion that objective truth (except this truth) does not exist. Also in the social world the only reality is unprincipled power, and there is no real difference between the two sexes: gender, like truth, is socially constructed, so there is no reason why women should not be priests if we do not dispense with priests altogether.

Many Catholic liberals were swept along as the older-style liberalism became entangled and confused with the more radical post-modern version, prompting Catholic conservatives to denounce liberalism of any stripe. They claimed that a toxic liberalism had invaded seminaries in the form of feminist nuns who discouraged so-called rigid candidates with the traditional view of sex roles.

Louis Putz hoped the Second Vatican Council's reforms would enhance the role of the laity in the Church. In that sense, he remained a liberal until he died. However, he had no interest in post-modernism. He was a 1950s type of liberal or reformer. An advocate of social justice and renewal in the Church, favoring Government programmatic activism of the New Deal, neo-Keynesian sort, poverty programs, Social Security, minimum wage, etc. But he also believed in something that might be termed post-post-modern: *that only the Church can provide "the vital energy to transform democracy into a true equality."* His solution was similar to Congar's: unity through a spiritual principle of order, not by a reductionist homogenization (the post-modernist's route) or bureaucratic power (the traditional Church's), nor by any leveling of the priesthood or of the hierarchy. The main problem to him always was cultural dualism, for which Catholic Action was the remedy. Since Catholic Action had become unfashionable and lost its constituency, he hoped Vatican II could do some of the job. But nothing would be easy.

By the time Fr. Putz exited Moreau Seminary it had become the premier model for seminary reform in the United States and elsewhere, having received wide exposure in newspapers and journals concerned about Catholic affairs in the United States. The next 30 years would make that an ambiguous legacy for some. But the two basic principles of his reform—that the laity is the key to the church's indispensable evangelizing mission, and that to assume its necessary role the laity must be prepared inside the church for leadership—is more relevant today than it was in 1965. Had Louis Putz not been on the scene at that time, the Catholic church's later travails might have been much worse than they actually were.

God is using us—He needs us to accomplish His work. This is
cause for great joy. Without our help, God cannot bring about the miracle that
He intends to effect in each one of us: through us but not without us.

Father Louis J. Putz, C.S.C.

He has given us this tremendous opportunity to be co-helpers with
God in the work of our own salvation, our own maturing process.

Father Louis J. Putz, C.S.C.

"As Catholics worthy of the name, we must be in harmony with
all of God's creation, with all of God's truth, in whatever race it may be
represented, in whatever creed it may be contained, and our effort
must be to discover it wherever it exists."

The Modern Apostle by Louis J. Putz, CSC (1957) p. 95

Chapter 7

New Heights

The last phase of Louis Putz's life was in some ways the most remarkable. In South Bend, as Putz was preparing to relinquish his duties at the seminary, a former student at his seminary, Frank Quinlivan, C.S.C, was working at a hospitality house for women and inadvertently played a key role in Putz's life. The diocese wanted to start a Human Development Commission and Quinlivan agreed to head it. He became friends with Msgr. John Reed, the head of Catholic Charities for the Diocese of Fort Wayne, which included South Bend. Knowing South Bend felt like a stepchild, Reed decided to open a Catholic Center in the city and bring all Catholic social services into it. He also wanted to start a family life program for the whole diocese and was looking for an administrator. Quinlivan told him Putz would be interested. Reed became excited and inquired, "Would he really do this?" Quinlivan also put Reed in touch with Roger Parent as a prospect to head Catholic Charities in South Bend.

At the farewell party the seminary held when Putz handed over the reins, Reed popped the question. He wanted Putz, as head of family service, to concentrate on the marriage preparation program, a role Putz had performed many years earlier in a program he had taken over from Theodore Hesburgh when the latter was appointed to the university administration. Like most lay-oriented Church programs, the diocese's marriage program slumped sharply in the 1960s, and Reed needed a rainmaker and reformer. With his additional experience with CFM, Putz was a natural and Bishop Pursley agreed to his appointment.

On the day Putz took up his new responsibilities, Msgr. Reed died of a heart attack, triggering a decline in the marriage program's financial support from the diocese. Putz salted the program with talks by friends who were recruited, logically enough, from CFM. The speakers and Fr. Putz expressed to the program attendees the exception they had to the hierarchy's rigid policy on birth control. Bishop Pursley decided that Putz's views were incompatible with the Church's sponsorship of the program and asked him to withdraw, but he generously invited Putz to continue with other duties. Pursley had listened to and been impressed by Putz's ideas on seniors, and happily seniors had little interest in the birth control issue. Putz turned his mind to the growing numbers of older people he encountered.

Many years later, Putz was asked by this writer why he had rejected Paul VI's encyclical, but Putz gave no firm doctrinal reasons. Instead, his response seemed rooted in his conception of Catholic Action's role. He thought Catholic Action should operate in specialized groups addressing secular problems related to their own specialty. These groups would then instruct the Church on the realities in the groups' spheres of competence to help the Church formulate policy in matters that related to the secular world. This was the best way to develop lay leaders in the Church. CFM's specialty was the family, and the birth-control commission was an almost perfect example of the correct approach. So Putz saw the Pope's rejection of the commission's advice as a debacle for his vision of the Church.

When asked that question, Putz was very old and had almost ceased to think in theoretical terms. He loved and respected the Crowleys and CFM members on the commission and believed they must be correct in their feelings of betrayal. Many who analyzed the encyclical found logical problems in Paul VI's reasoning. However, some state that Putz rarely expressed an opinion on clerical celibacy, women priests, or related issues, because he was little concerned about them. He never sorted such questions out, for he was consumed by the astonishing new organizing effort he was undertaking.

Charity, personal charity, is the master key that will open every heart. Here is a field of apostolate that lies at everybody's door. You need not be a powerful speaker to practice neighborly, Christian love; you need neither wealth nor position. On the Day of Judgment, Christ's sentence will not bear on your assistance at Mass, reception of Holy Communion, your fasts and abstinence, nor will good intentions be of any avail, these are means to an end, but it will call for your concrete acts of love.

Father Louis J. Putz, C.S.C.

Beginning in about 1966, Fr. Putz began to talk of CFM as primarily "about" families rather than changing society directly, in contrast to his earlier writings, in which he complained that "married people are often satisfied to limit their activity exclusively to the family." He was concluding that if Catholic Action's best days were behind it, CFM still could be a conduit to the hierarchy of lay insights on issues connected with the family. Therefore, he began to see CFM mainly as an instrument and expression of Vatican II rather than of Catholic Action, giving later liberal members some warrant to view their activities as a logical extension of Catholic Action.

Monsignor John Egan, whom Putz had brought to the seminary's staff, knew something about an abrupt change of career, and counseled Putz to enroll in a course of study and reflection to prepare himself for any such changes. At first reluctant, Putz finally became engrossed in the task and kept a journal as part of the course's requirements. The few surviving pages show him wrestling with two issues. The first had lurked behind Catholic Action from the start, but Catholicism's ghetto status had sheltered him from it. What exactly is the Church's proper stance toward the world? Now that Catholics were actually out in it, what should they do? What made the Unholy Trinity of secularism, materialism and individualism objectionable? Even Congar had said that the separation of sacred from secular institutions was a good thing. The modern economy freed many from desperate want, so why was this bad, if it was bad? The main western social tradition had always defended the rights and relative autonomy of the individual, and what was wrong with that?

With Catholics now out in the secular city, Putz could not avoid these questions. And if he couldn't, how was a lay person to figure out the answers? Can individual lay people, even if their mission is institutional and organized, make a dent in the problems? To begin to do so, wouldn't they need sustained and substantial institutional support? Characteristically, Fr. Putz wrote in the journal that he could derive more light from direct association with people in different activities than from abstract thought.

He knew that a lay person is shaped by the forces he or she is supposed to reform. But how does an individual come to understand her or his own personal journey in life? How do people learn to become aware of their own formative influences?

Putz wrote that institutions had become inhuman or dehumanized, and before one can hope to Christianize them, one must first humanize them, make them fully human. In this, we can cooperate with secular liberals and others. However, must we not first know how the institutions became dehumanized? Was it as a result of trying to separate them from religious and theological influences?

Must we not also clearly understand what it means to be human? On this issue secularists and theists were on a collision course, so cooperation might not be as easy and fruitful as he thought. Secularists had to become convinced that inhumane institutions were as much a danger to them as to anyone else.

Try as he did, Louis Putz could not penetrate to the core of this question. As he said earlier, the basic problem was cultural dualism. The only solution for that (as secularists understood) was, as Lincoln had said, to make society all one thing or all the other: secular(ist) or integrally theist. Any other solution was a delusion and a mirage, creating more problems than it solved. There was no possible middle ground, as many hoped. Compromises that worked legitimately for political purposes could only make the culture more conflicted and dissatisfying. And there can be no such thing as half a disciple. The modern age thought we should be wholly Christian only in some spheres of life or less than that in all of them. Catholic Action demurred. Its goal was to end the dualism in favor of Christian, or at least theist, culture. Exactly how to do that remained hidden from Louis Putz, and the goal of direct conversion urged on Catholic Action by the Popes ironically made Catholic Action miss the true solution, already implicit in it. But during Fr. Putz's next effort, one of his close associates would tease out the correct answer for him.

The Catholic Action truth, that there can be no middle way, no modus vivendi with secularism (not secularity), is the basic point of Putz's life. It may be an burdensome type of truth, as it was for many lay Catholics in the 1960s. A healthy society is theist, even if a theist society can be unhealthy. We cannot always avoid conflict and remain whole. Louis Putz's Catholic Action said in the simplest way that a good offense is not the best but the only defense. Rather than being an attack on anyone's rights, it is an assertion of truth. If you wait, you will be destroyed. Even the institutional Church found this idea inconvenient and ignored it. Many will not agree with it even now. But at least Putz's life can clarify the issue.

The second subject Putz broached in the journal he kept for the course was his interest in a new apostolate: the elderly, or what he called the "third age" of life (he picked up this term in France). His interest in it had been growing for about a year, and he had first mentioned it when he was 63 years old. (The targets of his interest were usually people of his own age—YCS and YCW in his youth, CFM in his middle age, and now seniors in his later years.) This last and long phase of Louis Putz's life may even be the most original and impressive, and exhibited an organizing energy not prefigured even by his earlier efforts in Catholic Action. Although he was not an intellectual in the standard sense, this stage also shows an intellectual dimension of exceptional purity and power.

When he went to work at Catholic Charities, Putz for the first time moved out of his Holy Cross community to live at an inner-city church, St. Augustine's. This was common at the time, as clergy reevaluated their lives in the secular city, and to a degree Louis Putz was simply keeping up. He began to organize discussion groups. Every Sunday night he brought into the rectory a clutch of people interested in a common subject. One night they were single women with children, and from this meeting an organization was formed that in turn gave birth to two more that are still in operation today. At his order's urging (possibly because the pastor quit and married), he moved out of St. Augustine's and joined Quinlivan at St. Patrick's and became increasingly interested in seniors. Many in the scattered army of senior citizens he encountered were subject to disabilities, but the vast majority were healthy, yet isolated. Pondering their condition, Putz saw regrettable anomalies.

On the Day of Final Reckoning Christ's sentence will not bear on your assistance at Mass nor on your fasts and self-imposed penances (these are means to an end) nor will good intentions as such be of any avail, but it will call for your concrete acts of love.

Father Louis J. Putz, C.S.C.

Borrowing the French terminology, he called these people "third agers." The first age ("learning") is youth (thus YCS), the second age ("earning") features the career (CFM), the third ("returning") is the time of retirement, or at least withdrawal from the career. Yet, there was this to consider: this age was generally defined negatively. The cohort of third agers was exploding in numbers and as a percentage of the population, and the baby boom would accelerate its growth even more. Meanwhile senior wellness was transformed by advances in medicine, economics, and nutrition, so that seniors were living more healthily and much longer. Their physical condition was often comparable to that of 40-year-olds of a century earlier, and the portion of a lifetime claimed by retirement was edging up from 25 percent to fully a third. Also, partly due to Social Security, seniors had become the nation's most affluent group, and a repository of huge untapped assets of experience, knowledge and continuing ability, not to mention cash.

Yet their cultural condition and status had not changed at all, and had even regressed. Although only five percent of third agers were institutionalized, and only another 15 percent were home bound, the image of the third age focused on them and ignored the healthy 80 percent. The third age was seen as a time of retrenchment and withdrawal, of senility, imbecility, "irregularity" and a perpetual search for "relief." Seniors' most creative act was shown on TV by drug companies to be indulgent chuckling over a grandchild. That image said much about the culture's veneration of youth, at whose shrine the aged were invited to worship so as to remain relevant. Society still applied to third agers the image of old age inherited from the 19th century.

Worse, the culture associated the seniors with death, a most dreaded reality that a secularist culture can see only as a dead end, a terminal horror from which it must recoil. As John S. Dunne wrote, the great question confronting post-modern culture is whether life is a becoming that leads to being, or does it lead to nothingness? If the latter, then the nothingness will infiltrate back into society, through the third age, and contaminate all of social life. Closer than others to the black hole, seniors could be tolerated so long as their wealth contributed to the economy, but otherwise the sooner they departed, the better. The extended family having vanished, adult children were less willing to take on the burden of retired parents, even when their own children had flown the nest.

Catholic Action, and by this we mean organized lay apostolate, is the modern layman's great opportunity for zeal. The need for Catholic lay leadership is great, its possibilities greater still, all of which caused Pope Pius XI to say repeatedly that the world will be saved only through Catholic Action with the layman assuming his responsibilities as a soldier of Christ, a fighting unit of the Church militant.

Father Louis J. Putz, C.S.C.

And seniors were internalizing the culture's crippling image which, emphasizing frailty and withdrawal, isolated them from each other and deterred them from creative activities other than golf and shuffleboard. But seniors collectively possessed many of the resources they needed; why should an older person living alone, for example, pay a commercial electrician for services a fellow retired electrician could provide for free? In addition, the service of helpful interaction was precisely what seniors needed most to sustain their inner vitality. Most crucial to the third age are relationships: an older person's network of relationships should not contract but expand! In fact, this was the age for breakout.

Just as he did with Catholic Action, Putz decided that secular society would never find the real solution on its own, nor would it depict this stage of life as a time for accelerated growth and expanded celebration. What—celebrate? The conjunction of celebration and dying well, Putz said, is crucial to the third age, because life really is becoming better. Detachment and withdrawal should create a new consciousness that jettisons earlier markers of status and replaces them with a new community of the spiritually mature across all classes. Aging people should not be imprisoned in their class.

The economy puts individuals on their own and demands aggressive activity in one's own behalf, even into the forties when adult psychology calls for mentoring and sharing. It thus inhibits personal growth and favors material accumulation, and makes "successful" people discontent while causing them to look forward to retirement, the conventional model of which will seal them into terminal frustration. Coming out of middle age, people today are less richly formed and developed than others were in earlier times. What people did not understand was that the new third age gave them a chance to recoup.

For this rise of the third age (resembling the rise of adolescence as a distinct phase a century earlier) kept alive the option of final fruition. A person emerging from the second age can activate the undeveloped portions of his or her personality, resolve lingering conflicts, and achieve real fulfillment—but only if the person engages and grows in a communal matrix. That is the great scandal. For society assumes that the third agers' goal and salvation is independence. To the contrary: the third-ager's salvation in this phase of life is renewed engagement and interdependence—and the more of the latter, the better! What third agers of earlier times derived from living with extended families, today's third agers must generate deliberately. For contrary to the conventional view, the distinctive issues of the third age are spiritual and not material, however grave the latter may be. Studied avoidance of the spiritual pins third agers into boxes and converts the boxes into tombs.

By this route, the senior cohort could considerably reduce the burden they put on society. Indeed, seniors could even make themselves the new integrating agent for a revived culture and polity—and not merely because their numbers grow. The polity has regressed into our conflict between interest groups coordinated impersonally by the economy. Even the State, earlier a key player, has had to subordinate its political to its economic role as a pawn of interest groups. Society badly needs a relatively disinterested moderator with no axes to grind. The senior group might qualify; already a swing factor in politics, its influence was mostly conservative, even reactionary. An active senior cohort still engaged in social problems and commanding resources to address them might become a more positive social force—the most positive creative force.

Who is our brother? Every man without exception! Our charity
must go out to all. The Mass is the great reservoir of charity. It binds us all to
God and to one another through Christ, the brother of all.

Father Louis J. Putz, C.S.C.

This was not to deny the approach of the Reaper. The third age brings us closest of all to God's own vulnerability. But the "narrow gate" to life is a deliberate decision for hope and action. The real problems of the third age can be solved only by and in a group. Even the wealthiest couples cannot escape the inner ravages of increasing age. Louis Putz's favorite example was Arizona's luxurious Sun City retirement community, which boasted the highest suicide rate of any area in the country. At any time, a spouse can face the sudden sickness of the other, forcing the couple either to strip itself of all assets so as to gain entry to a nursing home, or to accept imprisonment at home with the healthy spouse caring for his or her ill mate.

The Catholic Church had always pitched its strongest appeals to the young, and has poured resources into schools that train the intellect. However, its largest constituency is the aged people who built the schools and hospitals. They deserved some notice. Nevertheless, Putz was not thinking only of Catholics. He wanted to include all seniors.

When he arrived at Catholic Charities, his friend Harriet Kroll was there as an assistant to its first full-time director, Roger Parent, who was expanding its menu of services. Kroll was serving as key assistant to at least four energetic men. Catholic Charities shared an office with the other nominally separate group called Social Services, set up to qualify for aid from the United Fund. Parent was beginning a campaign to become mayor of South Bend, and many observers thought Kroll was doing most of the campaign work as well as Catholic Charities. (Parent remembers her particularly for her honesty and her proto-feminist consciousness: "...She did not like the subservient role imposed on women in the Church.")

Putz conceived a plan for a new organization to mobilize seniors, and he enlisted Kroll as his main assistant. He decided that, for several reasons, each group or chapter should be associated with a parish. The Holy Cross order operated at least 11 parishes in the city and this gave him a base. Parishes have heavy concentrations of seniors and the physical plant for meetings. Yet the new group also must be independent of the parish's direct control—the old principle from Catholic Action. The sell to the parish was that the new organization would serve the deepest needs of its largest constituency without loading new burdens on the parish.

Putz formulated a procedure for setting up each new group. First, he identified a parish with a large concentration of seniors, then compiled a list of about 30 names of those he could form into a leadership team. If the community already had leaders, they were included. At the first meeting, the group divided into three teams to brainstorm over the needs of the community's seniors and how they were being met. The entire group next reassembled, received reports from the teams, and elected an acting chair couple, who didn't need to be married to each other. It also selected an acting program chair couple and several committee heads. Finally it specified a date for the formal inauguration of the group, to which the acting officers sent invitations to all third agers in the area, and to the media. Putz called the new organization Harvest House.

We content ourselves with a legalistic and formalistic attendance
at Mass and reception of the sacraments without thoroughly investigating
the treasure we are juggling so irresponsibly.

Father Louis J. Putz, C.S.C.

The opening was a solemn affair, starting with a religious service followed by a social hour with light refreshments and a simple program of introduction. While some of the provisional leaders signed up new members, others circulated to create fellowship and conviviality. Finally, the acting chair couple announced the dates of the next leadership meeting and ensuing general meeting, to convey the message that Harvest House was on its feet and running. Within three months, the true leaders became apparent and democratic elections held.

Putz formulated five principles to guide the new movement. They were, in order:

Social awareness. To make society more aware of the rights and dignities to which accomplished third agers were entitled; and to apprise seniors of the causes of their oppression and thus to enlist them in the fight against injustice.

Service. Seniors should use their time and talents to support each other and society, recognizing the prominent collective dimension in their troubles and in the solutions to them.

Religious experience. However grave their material problems, third-agers' most basic problems are spiritual. Without a distinct spirituality, activity will be futile. Seniors can take the initiative on this themselves, but clergy often control the facilities they need to function.

Continuing education. A critical part of the spiritual dimension is constant learning, on which not just psychological but even physical vitality depend. Most social activities arranged for seniors are bland and tepid. Learning is the most powerful catalyst for sociality. (Putz would soon conceive a remarkable new way to address this.)

Community. Isolated action has little impact on society and even less on the individual person. All the basic problems of the third age are relational, and inner and outer strength lies in numbers. The experience and wisdom of seniors should echo in legislative chambers louder than their demands for money and services. Only united action could hope to influence government.

The chapter's monthly general meeting would focus on building community, and seek to open or exploit opportunities for communication, education, social service and the sharing of ideas. The exact blend would vary from chapter to chapter, but all chapters must try to implement each of the six points. An overarching bureaucracy was neither desirable nor necessary; the organization must arise from the grass roots and find its focus on the lowest level. Yet general coordination was vital to the chapters. The link among them would be an area Council composed of chapter chair couples, meeting monthly to exchange information for which it would be an important clearinghouse. One hired coordinator would perform administrative tasks that spanned all the chapters and regions. This person would have no power to install policies not welcomed by the chapters. (The responsibilities of this position fell, of course, to Harriet Kroll.)

Incarnation, Christ becoming one of us, is the great paradox of
Christianity. Christ has risen, but he wants to rise in each one of us. When this
happens because we seek Him, then we can count on Christianity succeeding.
The world will rise to a new life, to a new love, to a new resurrection—
in each one of us. Without prayer, without prayer that unites, there is no brotherhood. Let us lead the way to a new life in Christ, to recognizing
Him in our brother.

Father Louis J. Putz, C.S.C.

Putz recruited his old friend, Jim Armstrong, former head of the Notre
Dame Alumni Association and a member of St. Augustine's, to help
him form the first chapter. He recruited a Holy Cross nun, Sr. Gabriella
Doran, to organize the leadership team. Early in the Spring of 1973,
the solemn opening of the first Harvest House chapter occurred, with
Armstrong as president. Next, Putz persuaded another highly gifted
nun, Sr. Madeleine Adamczyk, S.S.J., to apply her huge talents to the
next chapter at St. Adalbert's parish. Then, laboriously but steadily,
Kroll and Putz formed new chapter after new chapter throughout
South Bend, Fort Wayne, and eventually elsewhere. Indianapolis soon
boasted a large membership. One of the most important responsibilities of the regional organization was to plan and prepare an annual or
biannual festival of celebration and fellowship, helping members to
see themselves as part of a significant movement. It was up to Harriet
to motivate people to produce these affairs, which eventually attracted
1,500 people. At first, the diocese sponsored Harvest House and fund-
ed a small budget.

After about a year, Putz had a new idea, perhaps the most astonishing
of his career. Alerted by his publishing experience to the importance
of ideas in creating movements, he saw intellectual stagnation as the
major danger in the third age. He identified intellectual growth as the
foundation of spiritual life. Somewhere in such mental activity lay the
nexus of spirit and society. So the need must be addressed directly in
a formal and organized way. Harvest House must create a new school
designed specifically for seniors; Putz set about to create it.

This project envisioned not only a new kind of school but a new and
huge plant and a complex organization. Putz succeeded, although the
new director of Catholic Charities, John Martin, refused to extend him
help with the project. Putz's first coup was to persuade Sr. Madeleine
to shift her attention from the St. Adalbert's Harvest House to the

new project. By all accounts, she was a highly gifted and energetic woman, and had held major offices in her order, which she persuaded to contribute its unused novitiate as the first home of the new school. The next problem was funding. Putz secured contributions in modest increments from a long list of religious orders (including his own) and foundations. Then he recruited an impressive faculty from among retired and active professors at local colleges and people with interesting skills, and finally he named the new school: the Forever Learning Institute (FLI). The faculty was to receive no pay; their reward was the service they performed and the pleasure of teaching an audience sincerely wanting to learn rather than merely occupy desks. The result was astounding: professors discovered that the classes were more stimulating and enjoyable than any they had ever taught, and some beat down the doors to return. They could express their true opinions and the students responded enthusiastically. There were no fixed curricula, no syllabi, no tests, no grades, no degrees to dilute or complicate the interaction. The learning greatly enhanced the sociality of the students and teachers. This was as close to heaven on earth as many of them would reach. Great themes, FLI proved, stimulate and enhance the mind and the social self much better than bland social events. FLI was a great success from its first day, when, expecting 40 students, it drew 115.

Putz teaching at Forever Learning Institute

The greatest evil of our times is the lack of adult education
in matters pertaining to religion.

Father Louis J. Putz, C.S.C.

The need for FLI had not been readily evident to anyone but Putz and its organizational requirements were enormous. He did not accomplish the task single-handedly, but the first-rate talent he attracted to it from the start makes it a bit mysterious. Even someone with a broad public image and following could hardly have done such a thing. Yet there it was. His creation of FLI renewed Louis Putz's reputation as a visionary and master organizer.

Even the formidable Harriet Kroll, lacking the proper credentials, could not perform the role of dedicated administrator of the forever learning institute and continue her work with Harvest House after Sr. Madeleine finally retired. FLI went through an administrator or two before it was fortunate to sign up a strong-minded Holy Cross nun who had served both as a high school principal and as a provincial superior of her order. She was Sr. Edith Daley, and she threw herself into the job, determined to maintain the highest standards. (Author's note: at this writing, Sr. Edith is still vigorously active at age 87 and seemed twenty years younger. She is warm, bright and cheerful.)

Spirituality reading is the more necessary today since our minds
are being continually bombarded with propaganda of the most insidious kind.
We must defend our minds against a steady flood of pagan maxims
and materialistic slogans glorifying standards and values diametrically
opposed to the Gospel.

Father Louis J. Putz, C.S.C.

FLI could not pay a large rental fee because it could not exact large fees from seniors. It even offered scholarships to some who could afford nothing. A memorial article in FLI's newsletter, *The FLI Sun* (October 1995), says that in about 1978, Bishop Pursley started a fund-raising appeal. Notes written by Louis Putz say that the fund-raising professionals hired by the diocese immediately recognized FLI as a major asset and counseled Pursley to include FLI in the promotional materials in order to borrow some of FLI's image and success. In return, Catholic Charities would help to fund FLI. When the host religious order in 1979 decided to sell the novitiate property after Sr. Madeleine's withdrawal, FLI moved to St. Patrick's empty parochial school. When it prospered, the pastor, Fr. Hoffman, asked for more rent, and FLI refused. Hoffman fired off a letter to the bishop denouncing FLI and Sr. Edith.

But Sr. Edith weathered his assault and FLI continued at St. Patrick's until it could find another location. Pursley died and was succeeded by Bishop McManus, who cut FLI's budget to a flat and pitiful $13,000 a year. The school now had to finance its own salaries and operations. Problems like this help to explain why other FLIs are so rare. Yet FLI and Harvest House prospered for the next 25 years—by 1985 the latter had 28 separate chapters in Northern Indiana alone, and 3,000 members—and are still flourishing at the time of this writing.

The arthritis from which Fr. Putz had suffered since his days as seminary rector had grown steadily. Extreme pain finally forced him into a wheelchair. Doctors pronounced that the disease was progressive and incurable and confronted him with the forced end to his career. They said he would never walk again and his religious superiors ordered him not under any circumstances to leave his residence, Corby Hall. The end of his active ministry seemed to have arrived.

But Putz conspired with a close friend to pick him up one morning at the back of the Corby residence. They set out in a car for a Montreal shrine called St. Joseph's Oratory, erected in honor of the Holy Cross order's main candidate for sainthood—a brother named André Bessette who was a fervent admirer of St. Joseph. Agony from his twisted limbs forced Putz and his friend to make repeated stops during the trip's long three days, until they arrived at the shrine on Labor Day, 1978. Fr. Putz immediately wheeled himself in, threw himself on the saint's mercy, and prayed for healing. After a while, he rose and they retreated to the place where they would find shelter for the night.

Fr. Putz said that at about 4 a.m. the following morning he experienced his familiar need to urinate. Half awake, he swung his legs over the bed and headed for the bathroom. As he approached it, he realized he was walking. He said that the next day he walked to the car. The trip home required 15 hours—and no stops. When he ambled into Corby Hall, the other priests were flabbergasted. The arthritis did not disappear completely for another year, but it steadily receded and finally vanished.

The healing became one of the official miracles required for Brother André's beatification, a consummation dear to the Holy Cross order's heart. After conducting three protracted and detailed examinations of the evidence, the Vatican's Sacred Congregation of Rites accepted the "medically impossible" healing of Fr. Putz as an authentic miracle attributable to Brother André, whom Pope John Paul II accordingly declared "Blessed" on May 23, 1982. Fifteen years later, at the age of 88, Putz still had the stance and sure-footed stride of a man thirty years his junior.

Putz had only begun. Word of what was going on in South Bend was spreading. In 1979, Bishop John Rauch of Phoenix, Arizona (where the concentration of seniors was much greater than in South Bend) invited Fr. Putz to perform a similar service for Catholic Social Services in that city. Putz was thinking of a national movement and decided to accept. His charge was to spearhead an FLI in Phoenix while implementing an existing six-points program for seniors, known as Senior Adult Neighborhood Groups (SANG). SANG presented the Harvest House concept with a limitation: sponsored by the diocese, it could not be independent. But it gradually created 20 chapters and 1,500 members.

A man named Sam Stanton who, beginning in 1982, worked for three years as Putz's personal assistant in Phoenix, says that the word that best describes the Putz he knew is "charismatic" because Putz so evidently believed in what he was doing. A man of ideas, he could hook people in to carry the ideas out. Putz organized several third-ager expeditions to Bavaria to learn about history (and to stay at a hotel run by his family). Stanton says Putz had an exceptional knack for dealing with uneasy situations and getting them to work out. A memorable moment was when Henri Nouwen came to town to give a lecture at a Franciscan retreat center. When Putz presented himself, the astounded Nouwen enthusiastically embraced Putz. Delighted to be reunited once more they went out taking Stanton along with them, to a nearby park to celebrate and talk. Many people have described Nouwen as charismatic, and they recognized this in each other. Putz also worked closely in Phoenix on third-age projects with another highly charismatic priest, Fr. Joseph Gremillion and together they organized numerous workshops. Stanton said that Putz and Gremillion were very close.

Unfortunately, before FLI could get much off the ground in Phoenix, Bishop Rausch died, robbing the project of a crucial backer, and SANG, to Putz's regret, was separated from the diocese. Putz stayed on in Phoenix's Catholic Social Services until June of 1984, while remaining busy elsewhere as well. With his help and that of a woman from Philadelphia, Vicky Peralta, Sr. Teresa Partin launched a new FLI in the Houston-Galveston diocese. Thus began a great friendship with Viky who went on in later years to join him on another senior project described later in this chapter. New Harvest Houses and FLIs rose up in Wichita, Kansas, with the support of Bishop Eugene Gerber.

In 1985, Harvest House and FLI in South Bend entered a crisis when Bishop McManus was succeeded by bishop John D'Arcy from Boston. The new bishop brought with him an administrator from Connecticut for Catholic Charities to give the organization new prestige. When Putz greeted the new bishop in the reception line after his installation, the bishop said, "So you're the fellow who ruined the seminary system." Oh, the thrill of ideological combat! The new administrator seized part of Harvest House's budget and installed her own person as head of FLI. Putz felt obliged to return to South Bend to reorganize nearly everything. He took Harvest House away from Catholic Charities and managed to secure support from an order of religious women. He termed it a "tough summer." The new diocesan administrator undercut Harriet Kroll and eventually forced her out.

It is not sufficient to know that the Church is in possession
of the right principles; these principles must be applied to each person's state
of life. It is difficult to see how this can be done without a good deal of
reading and study.

Father Louis J. Putz, C.S.C.

In 1988 Putz was ready to give up on his third-age ministry in Phoenix because of its new bishop's lack of interest and support. Putz received a call from Palm Desert, California, where his good friend, the talented Holy Cross priest Fr. Ned Reidy, had built the Christ of the Desert parish. Reidy had gone to the desert in 1980 to begin a new ministry to youth, college students and young adults at the College of the Desert in the Coachella Valley. He built up a Newman center at the college, but in 1988 he wanted to pursue a master's degree in theology, and asked Putz if he would take over his duties at the Newman Center. Putz consented, determined to extend the Harvest House movement to California. Christ of the Desert became his next home, between trips to South Bend, Wichita and Bavaria.

Of course, he looked for a new assistant, and again he hit the jackpot. At a South Bend seminar he had become more familiar with the formidable Vicky Peralta, founder of a gigantic and hugely successful service to seniors, named Project: HEAD, in Philadelphia. It later spread to New Jersey, Baltimore and Washington, D.C. After immigrating from the Philippines to the United States in 1962, Peralta was the American Director of the Social Services Work Center under the Jesuit Mission. She was a Fulbright scholar, who created, almost from nothing, the enormous and original Philadelphia organization (much resembling Harvest House) which gained her world-wide recognition for her work with seniors. Putz visited Peralta and her husband, Dan, at their retirement home in Malaga, Spain. One night at dinner, he innocently suggested that she think about going with him to California to launch a new series of Harvest Houses. Everyone laughed at this "silly idea." But Putz had read his friend well; the seed took root. She called him after a few weeks to discuss the proposition, and before Dan knew what had happened, the couple was living in a new home near Palm Desert. Putz often lauded the 60-year-old Peralta as a talented and powerful personality.

Peralta has written a brief memoir of her work together with Putz. Between the lines of an affectionate tribute to her mentor, one can read the story of an epic struggle. Every morning, she and Putz girded themselves for an approach to a new parish or a new audience. The proposition was unfamiliar and at first struck few sparks in the prospects. Peralta writes of days of Herculean labor that was little rewarded. Frequently, she became demoralized and depressed, but Putz remained upbeat and pushed the pace. They went out early and arrived home late, when Dan was already in bed, and sometimes they took their dinners in seedy roadside eateries. But slowly the effort gained traction; gradually they refined their message to reach a California audience and new chapters began to accumulate: at the Newman Center, at Our Lady of Soledad (Coachella), Our Lady of Perpetual Help (Indio), St. Louis (Cathedral City), St. Elizabeth (Desert Spring), Our Lady of Guadalupe (Mecca). Harvest House was being born again in the California Desert.

On audio tapes from those days, in which Putz discusses his work, one hears again the semi-hypnotic allure in his voice. The success of most tapes results from the speaker's aggressive individuality and ego. There is none of this in Putz. His voice has neither inflection nor emphasis, but undulates swell-like in long rises and falls. In this voice, one begins to catch a glimpse of some long-sought home. An actor who could duplicate this effect might make his career and fortune, but it may be impossible. His tape interlocutors did not want the conversations to end, even after they had exhausted their questions. What captured one's attention in his voice was his manner—a quietude and repose, as if, wholly present to the moment, he were settling in for a long conversation that no call, however urgent, would interrupt. A sort of expansive blessedness hit one with almost physical force.

The tapes reveal Putz's sensitivity to the nuances of the local environment. They show that his indifference to abstract organizational planning was offset by a sort of genius at working out the details of particular relationships and connections unique to each location. So, the chapters that he and Peralta managed to form were enduring, strong, yet individually distinctive. One was filled with Mexicans intent on service to the local community; another was teeming with elderly focused on the disabled, while the Newman Club Harvest House chapter was replete with seasonal transients from the East and North and concentrated on intellectual development. This group had an odd problem: it was so closely linked to the college that its members saw little need of either a separate Harvest House or an FLI. Putz always insisted on establishing a new FLI wherever he went, but ever adaptable, he worked out a compromise in which FLI supplemented the courses the local seniors took in force at the college. All were satisfied.

It was in the Coechella Valley that Louis Putz encountered a man who, in the Hispanic community, exemplified (unbeknownst to Putz) Catholic Action. The Holy Cross mission in the Coechella had been started in 1973 by another Holy Cross priest improbably named Jose Pawlicki. Having worked for a long time in Texas he had come to know and deeply love the Mexicans he met there. He saw that the standard American approach to parishes had no appeal for them. They wanted and needed communities based on relationships, not mere functions. So Fr. Pawlicki began to think that the famous "base" communities of South America might have part of the answer. When invited by a bishop to work in the Coechella, Pawlicki declared his intention to try to form such communities there and was not refused. He set to work and was soon joined by several more Holy Cross priests. Guided by experience, Pawlicki formulated specifications for a base community, of which two are directly relevant to Catholic Action. First, before joining a group, a prospect must undergo a conversion during three days of actually living in a community. Second, the main purpose of the community is not action but relationships. Any action results from them. In other words, Pawlicki subordinated the Catholic Action observe-judge-act "methodology" (of which he was well aware) to the primary relationships within the group. Before very long, the group of

Holy Cross priests had 30 base communities functioning among 5,000 families with some 18,000 Hispanic Catholics.

The significance is that community-building comes before all else. No other goal can come before it because it is the most essential mark of Christian life. While he may not have known it at the time, Pawlicki was doing something desperately needed by a vastly wider population. He was able to do it because, working with Hispanics, he was not confronted with the ideological complexities of American culture. It is significant that Louis Putz, the 20th century American priest most dedicated to fostering social activism among Catholics, wrote as almost his final testament that a goal of Catholic Action and forming communities must always go together.

> Not only does God respect our individual natures, but
> even our social character. We must not only save ourselves, but save
> one another. Again, we have the mutual relationship of brotherhood,
> our corporate-ness brought home to us.
>
> Father Louis J. Putz, C.S.C.

On the tapes, Putz paints a vivid picture of the local church. The Catholic Charities of the San Bernardino diocese did not support Harvest House, so he was dependent on and at the mercy of the local pastors, most of whom were Irish-born transplants imported by an earlier bishop of San Diego and intent on making money they could remit to the old sod. They had been transferred wholesale to a new San Bernardino diocese when it was split off from San Diego, and they were highly resistant to outside "interference" unless they needed help. They did not generally welcome Harvest House. They account for much of the resistance Putz and Peralta met. In contrast, the pastors who were members of orders were highly receptive. Most of the local pastors, whether "secular" or "religious," were less educated than the university-trained Holy Cross priests, including Putz, who had gradually congregated in the area. They were far more competent to work with specialized groups, such as youth and seniors, that the diocese needed to serve. Putz envisioned a Holy Cross mission to the local Mexicans that would be "the most powerful Hispanic apostolate in the world." As he said, in Palm Desert he became engrossed in far more than Harvest House and the Newman Club. It seemed that the valley in which Palm Desert lay should itself become a new diocese, in which the Holy Cross order could assume a leading role—or so he thought.

Harvest House and FLI might have grown faster and more widely than they did if it were not for Putz's neglect of publicity and promotion. He sometimes wrote articles, but the prose was only workmanlike and failed to highlight the movement's unique character and importance. In his seeming dearth of ego, he generally sought to shift the credit to others, and this contributed hugely to his local successes but hurt his efforts to publicize or dramatize the movement.

In addition, the specific qualities of any Harvest House chapter were set by its local environment, and this required an adaptability and re-sourcefulness that few possessed in so large a measure as did Putz. Ergo, his frequent presence was needed at each local installation. A well-constructed set of promotional materials and organizational instructions might have offset this limitation, but such were never developed—perhaps for budgetary and time constraints.

However, the main obstacle was Harvest House's chronic dependence on social service bureaucracies such as Catholic Charities. (Author's note: these oftentimes fickle charities had their own agendas and needed to take credit for and control of any operation they sponsored.) Harvest House required reliable sources of independent financing, but as a "spiritual" operation, it was anathema to conventional secular funders and its autonomy made it indigestible to many bureaucratic Church sources.

Harvest House's survival and gradual growth depended on Putz's ability to overcome reversals and betrayals that should have been devastating to the organization. What saved it was his unique vision, his incredible organizing energy sustained well into his eighties, his profound sensitivity to the peculiarities of a situation, his unmatched ability to attract and motivate talented people and, above all, his ability to energize them to work together toward a common lofty goal. No amount of organizational planning could have compensated for defects in these areas, and any revival of Harvest House should begin with a close study of Putz's methods of creating it. It would have been a singular achievement for any person to have formed one Harvest House, not to mention an FLI. He created dozens. Wherever he went, the movement followed and succeeded. That achievement should be replicable by less remarkable successors.

"It is significant, indeed, that Our Lord always compared heaven to a banquet. What better way to describe community."

The Modern Apostle by Louis J. Putz, CSC (1957) p. 36

Chapter 8

Last Years and Days

In 1992, Louis Putz transferred the full responsibility for Harvest House in California to Vicky Peralta and returned to live at St. Paul's Retirement Community in South Bend, from which he resumed his work there with Harvest House and The Forever Learning Institute. A hand-written note in Putz's papers reads that the mayor of Palm Desert told him drug lords had a contract out on him and that he needed to leave town immediately. For whatever reason, Putz appears to have ceased his efforts to spread Harvest House to new locations and to have shifted into a maintenance mode. The reason he gave for returning to South Bend was that a new director at Catholic Charities wanted to change FLI's leadership. The director steeply downgraded three of the five activities performed by Harvest House and FLI. When Putz resisted, the diocese canceled its sponsorship.

Beginning in 1986, Putz often told friends he wanted to start an autobiography and a "revolutionary" new book on the theology of the laity's place in the Church. He was thinking about his legacy. During the years after 1992 he worked on both writing projects, but his progress was slow; he had never been an especially good writer. But transcripts of dictated notes from these years are full of arresting details.

A document he wrote titled "The Place of the Laity in the Catholic Church" was probably a sketch for his contribution to the revolutionary theology of the laity. It attributes the decline in clerical vocations to the Church's continuing clericalism. The Vatican attacked theologians who disagreed with it, including many women theologians. Its clericalist bias resulted from the Council of Trent's focus on seminaries, Putz wrote. Although Vatican II recognized that the laity demanded and needed close collaboration with the hierarchy, the hierarchy suspected that this would threaten its own interests. But to perform any leadership role in the world the laity must develop its leadership skills within the Church, and what is truly at stake here is the Church's role in the world. The continuing dismissal of the laity is by far the Church's greatest flaw, he wrote. The document describes several instances in which lay initiatives were sabotaged by the hierarchy.

According to Putz's document, what the Church badly needs is a model for bringing lay leadership into the councils of the Church, if only for consultation. JOC offers a model; it revolved around small leadership groups that were missionary and lay in their orientation—two features key to any solution. To meet its own needs, as arguably Trent did in training priests better for the clerical state, the Church must now build up the laity. The hierarchy is suspicious, but it must realize that it is not the laity that has failed.

In place of the correct form of consultation with the laity, the official Church has embraced a reactionary model created by an organization named Opus Dei, founded by José Escriva, a Spanish priest whom Pope John Paul II beatified. This group operates in secrecy and its leaders are upper-class conservatives (the Vatican's best replacement for the aristocracy) in banking, law and medicine. A priest is in charge of each group, while its head is a bishop who reports only to the Pope. Doctrinally, Opus Dei is extremely conservative and opposed to ecumenical dialogue. Its founder was hostile to Vatican II and to Pope John XXIII's ideas. According to Putz, even Cardinal Ratzinger (the Church's present pope) indicated that the founder's beatification came "too quickly."

In this same document, Putz writes that Call to Action might be a good counterweight to Opus Dei. It is a lay movement controlled by graduates of earlier Catholic Action organizations who welcomed Vatican II. In any case, generally lacking in North America are broad lay-based groups dedicated to the formation of lay Christian leadership. The South American "communities de base" may be a promising model, but the hierarchy sees them as a threat to its clericalist style.

In another hand-written paper from those days, "Why the Importance of the Laity in the Church?" Putz sketches out some reasons for why church officials felt threatened. The Vatican II document on the Constitution of the Church established the equality of laity with clergy, but the Church has never been organized on that basis. The causes of the new emphasis are that the laity is highly educated, while society is democratic (and controlled not by authority but by public opinion), scientific, industrial and specialist. The Church lacks structures to fit this society. It is highly centralized, autocratic and paternalistic, and its very means of communication date from the era of absolutism. Vatican II tried to set new trends in motion by becoming open to discussion, dialogue and respect for people and their competence. Specialized movements are critical to any renewal. Needed now is a lay spirituality as well as priest assistants to the laity—rather than the other way around. According to Putz, the Church needs an apostolate to the temporal order, with lay people taking initiative within their walks of life, being formed through action rather than monastic retreat, supported by the liturgy, missionary in their emphasis, and organized (all ideals of Catholic Action).

In a third document, "The Way of the Cross," Putz wrote an outline for his autobiography. It describes his life as a story of separations: from his mother, from early classmate friends, from the Sternals, the Carricos, the graduating class at Notre Dame, from France, and finally from the Kroll family. This coloration may throw light on a characteristic observed much earlier by Vince Giese (in an article, "Chaplain to the Working Apostolate," *Today*, November, 1954): Putz's detachment from his projects and leaders. Giese attributed this detachment to Putz's noble desire not to gather personal followers, because his goal was group experience, not personal aggrandizement. But the biographical sketch suggests that the detachment might have hidden a wound in Putz's personality, and might help to explain why he was able to form new attachments and to walk away from them. The same wound might even have invited the rebuff that later shortened his life.

In 1996, Putz moved into Corby Hall, the main priests' residence on the Notre Dame campus, from which he continued to work with Harvest House and The Forever Learning Institute in South Bend. The hall bears the name of a president of Notre Dame who achieved fame as chaplain of the Union army's celebrated Irish Brigade in the Civil War. Corby addressed his soldiers, the "fighting Irish," just before they blunted Longstreet's assault on the Wheatfield at Gettysburg. He gave general absolution but instructed that there would be no absolution for cowards who failed to do their duty. Even some Protestants then accepted absolution. A few days later, many of these soldiers were sent, exhausted, to put down other fighting Irish in the New York City draft riots. Corby is the only Civil War chaplain memorialized by two statues. One stands on the great battlefield, not far from where he exhorted the troops. The other is in front of Corby Hall, which thus reeks of American and Catholic tradition, echoing Notre Dame's motto: "God, Country and Notre Dame."

At Corby, Putz began casting about for help with his writing. Harriet Kroll was in no physical condition to assist. (Author's note: when she died in 1997, Putz said he had lost "...his right arm.") He also began to look for a successor, whom he hoped would be a lay person. It was early in 1997 that he asked me, almost a chance acquaintance, to help him. Apart from his work with Harvest House and FLI, he was not visibly doing anything else of much note. But he often played his cards close to his vest. On frequent visits, I went with him on his rounds and spoke to many people who had long known him, and I gradually gained an awareness of his life and work. He was faithful to a vigorous exercise program, swimming several times a week in the St. Mary's College pool. Because his appreciation of writing projects was much on his mind I talked to him long and often.

He also inserted me onto the board of an organization about which I knew little except that it had been started by Putz and a group of senior Notre Dame graduates who wanted to mobilize third-age members of the Notre Dame family to engage in service to society by pooling their talents together, and help solve social problems in their home towns. He faithfully attended the meetings of this board, and behaved in his usual way. During meetings that were often long and tedious, he said virtually nothing and even appeared to doze. He observed his principle that the priest must not take charge, and he knew that all groups must go through a certain process to become productive. But when a liturgy began he sprang to life and delivered strong, galvanizing homilies that assured us we were engaged in an historic effort with large implications for the Church and society.

This group, then named "Notre Dame's FIRST" (Fighting Irish Retirement Service Team), was sponsored by the Notre Dame Alumni Association, through its community service program. The name was later changed to Notre Dame Senior Alumni.

The group which became Putz's last hurrah for his beloved church had been started by Putz, another charismatic senior, Gene Slevin from the Notre Dame Alumni Association and Chuck Lennon, the executive director of the Association. Lennon, years earlier, had incorporated community service into the mission of the Association and each geographic Notre Dame Alumni Club. This thrust was recognized by and received accolades from the educational community nationally.

A proven volunteer, Gene Sullivan hosted the first meeting in Joliet, Illinois, where two subsequent organizational meetings were also held and hosted by Joe and Jodie Adler. Father Putz came from South Bend and brought with him Isabel Charles, Dean Emeritus of the College of Arts and Letters, and Walt Collins, former editor of the *Notre Dame Magazine*. George and JoAnn Harvey came from Decatur, Alabama and were the only non Notre Damers in the original group. They met Fr. Putz at the Notre Dame Fatima Retreat Center discussing social concerns and outreach projects back in Decatur. Putz liked what he saw and immediately brought the Harvey's on board the new "FIRST"

Fighting Irish Retired Service Team. All involved in the initial meetings would enthusiastically look forward to the liturgies with Fr. Putz as celebrant. It was as if they all felt like they were concelebrants. There were themes for each liturgy. The Eucharist was taken together as one. The dialogue homilies and petitions involved local, national, and international problems. The openness of the group brought out personal prayer requests. Interesting enough Putz chose women more than men to be proclaimers of the word.

All would gather in a semi-circle for the liturgy of the word and then right around the alter for the Eucharistic celebration. Adler and Harvey would become chairmen of FIRST. Later the Harvey's would receive honorary alumni status. At mass with Fr. Hesburgh, there have been only 29 recipients in the history of Notre Dame. All involved were deeply moved. Their expertise was most valuable in this effort. Those present at the Joliet meeting became members of the initial board.

Putz, always the innovator, stressed that the Fighting Irish Retired Service Team enter into a ministry for "Third Agers," a term he preferred to "senior citizen" or "golden ager." He borrowed the phrase from French social scientists who see life as a chain with three links: the age of learning, the age of earning, and the age of returning. The last being that point in life where there's time to give back accumulated knowledge, talent and experience to society's needy members.

FIRST group poses with Fr. Hesburgh after Mass in his office

The Association was not receptive to the argument of some on the board, at first a somewhat random collection of people accumulated because of their service background, that the third age's special characteristics required a different approach reflecting the features of a movement rather than an organization. The Alumni Association was definitely the latter. Putz saw FIRST as a possible third age break-through, because its members were professional, self-starting and intelligent.

NDSA before working in South Bend Food Pantry

During his final two years, Putz displayed unflagging vitality and great joy in mingling with his beloved lay seniors. They did not defer to him or treat him as special, but they shared a warm familiarity. He expressed over and over a great disappointment: that in all his years in Harvest House he had never been able to interest his third-agers in social service. (Author's note: he was excited about FIRST because it might fill that gap. Under prodding, Harvest House third-agers took some, but little, interest in politics, and almost none in service proj-ects to others than themselves. He thought that, in South Bend at least, this reflected the characteristics of the tight-knit, inward-direct-ed ethnic groups, few of whose members were highly educated. Others thought it might be a reflection of their class. I thought the problem went deeper. Service orientation requires people to reverse patterns imposed on them over a lifetime. Survival for these people has re-quired their focused attention to their own finances and on expecting little help from others, even the members of their local communities. People cannot follow one principle in that respect and another when they engage life "religiously." Insulated as he was from financial pres-sures, Fr. Putz never fully gauged the importance of the economic is-sue in the lives of Americans.)

Putz had not declined physically very far before an exhilarating inter-lude occurred. I spoke to him about what Catholic organizations he saw as legitimate successors to Catholic Action. He said that the most likely candidate was Call to Action, a liberal (and almost post-modern) group. I said that it was concerned mainly about internal Church reform and had little of Catholic Action's interest in evangelizing. I asked what he thought of the Chicago group named The National Center for the Laity. He had never heard of it. I explained that it was concerned with the Catholic laity's mission to the world and seemed to have no stake in the liberal-conservative mud wrestle. When he heard that the legendary Ed Marciniak was backing the National Center, his ears perked up and he wanted to know more. I told him about the center's gifted editor, Bill Droel, who produced the exceptional newsletter called *Initiatives*. Putz asked me to make an appointment for him with Droel and drive him to the meeting.

A few days later the three of us met at a Chinese restaurant in Oak Park, just West of Chicago. We began with the usual pleasantries, and Putz seemed relaxed. But suddenly he sat forward in his chair, his body stiffened, and he fired off a staccato series of sharp questions at Droel. As startled as I was, Droel pulled back an inch or two but then stood, toe to toe, with Putz and gave as good as he got. The questions and answers flew so fast that I could not record them, but Putz was feeling out Droel about the prospect of organizing, and he meant business! The old lion was ready to roar one more time. In those few moments he radiated power. But when he saw that Droel had no intention of organizing, Putz resumed his earlier manner. I had never seen him respond in that way, but now I understood him better.

The greatest institutions of America have not been its banks.
The greatest buildings in America have not been its skyscrapers. The greatest institutions and the greatest buildings of America have been its homes, scattered across our beautiful countryside or clustering by the thousands upon the acres of our crowded municipalities.

Father Louis J. Putz, C.S.C.

Of course, what Putz suggested was impossible, but how unfortunate. If this meeting had occurred 20 years earlier, how different everything might have been. Fr. Putz might have shown Droel how little he was likely to accomplish without some organizing drive, and Droel might have been the "communicator" Fr. Putz needed. But on that day the old lion fell silent for good.

Putz's papers also show that his removal from Corby interrupted a project that might have had fateful results: the planning for the "revolutionary" book on the laity's place in the Church was well along. He and his collaborator, James Michael Lee, were sketching out chapters that would ramify the theme in many areas, such as canon law, ecclesiology, history, biblical theology, and so on. They had decided on experts for about half the chapters, and Putz was to write the lead chapter, as a touchstone for the authors of the others. But the sudden decline in his health put a stop to everything.

Attached to a prospectus that the two editors intended to send to prospective collaborators was an outline of chapter one that Putz was to write. That outline follows almost verbatim:

> The laity are the Church. Laypersons are just as fully Church as are the clergy and the hierarchy. Laity, clergy, and hierarchy are not descriptors of a state of either intrinsic or objective ecclesial superiority, but rather descriptors of functions within the Church. The ecclesia is not the clergy or hierarchy exclusively, and ecclesiology is not cleric logy or hierarch logy.

> The laity should be the principal functional and canonical arm to accomplish the Church's basic mission, namely to Christianize the world. In this authentic perspective, the role of the clergy and the hierarchy is primarily to assist the laity to perform this Christianizing mission successfully. Thus the laity do not have an ancillary role in the Church. On the contrary, it is the clergy and the hierarchy who have the ancillary role. Put directly, the fundamental task of the clergy and the hierarchy is to serve the laity both as persons and as apostles.

> The old two-tiered model of the Church's mission in the secular world and the religious world is fundamentally flawed. This defective model posited that the clergy and the hierarchy run the religious world while the laity operate in the secular world (typically at the bidding of the clergy and hierarchy). A correct and authentic ecclesial model holds that both the religious world and the secular world are the direct province of the laity, and that the laity should direct both of these arenas, with the assistance of the clergy and the hierarchy.

> Subsidiarity is a key functional principle in the Church. If the laity can accomplish any given task, then they should. Thus the only tasks in

which the clergy and hierarchy should be involved are those mandated by both The Great Commission (Mt 28: 19-20) and the priestly ordination ceremony, namely sacramental functions and religious education functions (religious instruction and pastoral counseling). Even here the principle of subsidiarity obtains.

The laity must be given their genuine decision-making tasks. Up to now, the clergy and the hierarchy have blocked the decision-making role of the laity. They contend that the laity are just supposed to pray, pay, and obey.

The history of the Church, e.g., the early Benedictines, has shown that early in ecclesiastical history the task of the clergy was to assist the laity in exercising the latter's prime role in the Church.

From the Dark Ages onward, the clergy took advantage of the fact that the laity by and large were relatively uneducated. Thus, they took ecclesiastical power unto themselves as an excuse to compensate for the generally uneducated laity. Now that the laity are educated (sometimes more so than the clergy and the hierarchy) there is no longer a valid excuse that the clergy and hierarchy have to run the Church by default.

The liturgy should be more lay-oriented both in important liturgical decisions and in major liturgical participation.

The canonization process must be overhauled. As of now there is a tremendous in-built bias against the laity being raised to sainthood.... members of religious orders get their deceased members canonized because they have the person power and the funds to advance the process. Yet the laity need lay role models in their path to sanctity. And the laity need recognition for their quiet lives of Christian discipleship and often of heroism.

In conclusion, the emphasis in the Church should be on community, the equality of fellowship between lay and ordained persons all doing their job to Christianize the world. There really cannot be a true community of apostleship when a relatively small number of persons give the orders and the rest of the community (laity), simply because they occupy a particular canonical state, are required to passively and sometimes sheepishly follow these orders.

Several months after the Oak Park meeting, Putz suffered a fatal stroke. The night before the funeral at a celebration following mass in Moreau Seminary, many of his friends spoke publicly about his life and influence on their lives, which for them the meeting seemed a love-fest. I will wait to celebrate, however, until his legacy is firmly established.

Fr. Putz now rests in a consecrated grave with other Holy Cross priests devoted to our church.

Thoughts....

At the wake at Moreau Seminary the evening before Father Putz's funeral, Father David Burrell, whose friendship with Father dated back to his student YCS days at Notre Dame, led the prayers and the reflections and remembrances of those who wished to share their stories about Father Putz.

The following moring, the celebration of Father Putz's life was held at Sacred Heart Basilica. The Church was filled with his friends, fellow priests, ex-students, and people from all the Movements that he had been involved with throughout his life. At the Offertory, representatives from these groups presented mementos marking their connection with this remarkable chaplain. One of the people attending the funeral remarked that it was the first time in her memory that a woman had been permitted to do one of the readings at the funeral of a priest.

There was a sense of loss at the death of a beloved mentor and friend, but also a sense that he had left a challenge for those in the pews to continue to work for justice and social change. The funeral ended with everyone walking from the Basilica to the Holy Cross priests' cemetery and final prayers at the gravesite.

"The problem of our separated brethren, the problem of racial and national and international feuds, is a problem of the Church......
Christ's membership includes all races, all people. The Church must reach them all."

The Modern Apostle by Louis J. Putz, CSC (1957) p. 22

Appendix A

Awards and Recognition

"A national leader in the Catholic Action movement, Fr. Louis Putz began working with Young Catholic Workers while in France. During his teaching years at Notre Dame, he directed the National Federation of Catholic College Students and founded Young Christian Students as well as the Christian Family Movement. In the 1970s, Fr. Putz founded Harvest House and the Forever Learning Institute, places of social relaxation, spiritual enrichment and continuing education which have been replicated across the country... Fr. Putz is the author of several books on the church, seminary education, apostolic action, and the spirituality of aging."

Father Louis Putz *Vita*

A.B. University of Notre Dame, 1932

Grand Sem, Le Mans, France, 1932-35

S.T.B., Catholic Institute, Paris, France 1936

Hon. LL.D., University of Portland, 1959

Hon. D.H., St. Mary's College. 1970

Assoc. prof. of Theology, Notre Dame, 1940-66

Rector Moreau Seminary, Notre Dame, 1966-72

Director Catholic Action and President Fides Publishers, Notre Dame, IN 1957-79

Founder and Director Harvest House 1973

Founder and Executive Director of the Forever Learning Institute, 1974

Founding Board Member of the Notre Dame Senior Alumni

Recipient of:

"**Reinhold Niebuhr**" Award at University of Notre Dame, 1975, for outstanding contribution to work in the field of aging.

The Dr. Thomas A. Dooley Award

Presented by the University of Notre Dame

Alumni Association

January 27, 1995

Honorary Doctorate

From the University of Notre Dame

May 1988 and citation

Dr. George E. Davis Award

For noteworthy Ministry with the Aging

Presented to Louis J. Putz, C.S.C.,

October 22, 1986

Fort Wayne, Indiana

From the 1986 Governor's Conference on Aging by The Interfaith Fellowship on Religion and Aging

---

The Rev. Louis J. Putz, C.S.C., Senior Service Award

Established in 2002 by the Notre Dame Alumni Association

Recognizes senior alumni and friends who have developed and implemented programs that have made significant contributions to improving the lives of others.

Appendix B

Excerpts from Fr. Putz Writings on Laity

Homily for the Golden Jubilee Mass of Rev. Louis J. Putz, C.S.C.

By Rev. David Burell, C.S.C. (1986),

Like Elijah in today's reading, Louis is a human being like ourselves—indeed, that is what endears him to so many. As a student at Notre Dame in the famous 50's, I knew that one of its claims to fame was that a Holy Cross priest lived on each floor of every residence hall. Most of us found most of them redundant, but Louis was different. He had a way of transcending the place—which has habitually indulged in celebrating itself in a kind of inward-looking lock step. Louis, by contrast, was busy exploring international connections, wrought through pre-war years of theological study in France, to bring the latest in strategical pastoral thinking to America— indeed, to the Midwest. Yet he also appreciated the place—its students and the faculty, and was ever appreciative of the opportunities for initiatives and for ministry which the spirit of Holy Cross afforded him.

Part of Louis' secret, explaining what made him different, was that his studies in France had in fact put him in touch with the sources of Holy Cross spirit—the sources which had animated the imagination of Father Moreau himself. He told some of us, on one occasion, that he had set himself to read Costes' 3–5 volume biography of St. Vincent de Paul during his deacon year. And the "apostle of the poor," as his own writings testify, had imbibed the very best of the French school, and turned it into action. That example would shape Louis Putz's entire life: to take the best of current theology and spiritual reflection, and turn it into action.

As would the quality of resolve which had set such a task for a deacon year. Instead of contenting himself with what comes, or accepting a fixed agenda, Louis seemed impelled to expand horizons—his own and others'. It was such an intellectual vision, explicitly linked to a program of formation-through-action, which captured our imaginations in that otherwise complacent era. The winds of change were sporadic breezes at Notre Dame in those days, fanned by Father John Cavanaugh's friendship with Robert Hutchins and a few stimulating faculty—mostly laymen—and circulated among students by a group animated by Louis Putz, with the assistance of a handful of Holy Cross priests and brothers who also sensed something stirring. Among these were Joe Haley, Charlie Harris, "Doc" Kenna, Ted Hesburgh, and Brother Lawrence, as well as enterprising Holy Cross sisters like Agnes Cecile, Maria Renata, and Charles Borromeo. What these chaplains and moderators helped to model in their YCS groups was a church whose shape would emerge at Vatican II as the "people of God." Hierarchy turned itself inside out to catalyze lay involvement, and the result was an interacting group of peers seeking ways to shape their lives and their actions by a new-found sense of the gospel.

What would soon be celebrated by social theorists from Frankfort to the New School in New York as a new logic for understanding society—we learned from the inside-out in those ragged little groups. Louis' early disappointment (that his desire to study history was declined by a civil engineer turned Provincial) became our gain, as his intellectual virtuosity turned to molding YCS groups, and his entrepreneurial and risk-taking propensities led him into publishing—mostly translating as well—current works of theology touting an exciting return to Christian sources and to a vital, living faith... "nouvelle theologie."

All this by way of introduction to a many-sided person whom all of us here know and love, yet each from a slightly different angle. I have emphasized the relentlessly inquiring spirit, doubtless because that is one of the things I have most admired in him, but also to remind us how any faithful follower of Jesus will be led in his or her life to reconcile what the world divides. "Activist" and "intellectual" are often opposed one to another, but there is no reason why a person of God cannot combine the two—as did M. Vincent and as does Louis Putz. The result is a "human being like ourselves," who inspires a calm trust in the working of the Holy Spirit together with a restless yearning to have a hand in completing that very work. Such a one finds Jesus' openness to all comers—children especially—"the most natural thing in the world" and simply cannot comprehend the apostles' "proto-clerical" reaction. Similarly congenial is James' insistence that the community surround each suffering member with its solicitude— the text used to craft later sacramental teaching on the "sacrament of the sick"—and so display the fruitfulness of the gospel in our lives.

Nor can that fruitfulness remain an individual gain—it must be distributed to others—widely, from South Bend to Chicago, and indeed "to the ends of the earth." The gentle yet forceful presence of the Lord-become-a-living-Spirit—what Elijah experienced on the mountain of the Lord, Louis has helped us discover in the midst of our work, and now beyond what the world calls "work"—into the "third age" of "senior citizens." What is the secret? I suggested a tapping of the very sources of Holy Cross spirit—in St. Vincent de Paul; but that source needs in turn to well up within each one of us—as we faithfully return each day to drink deeply of the wells of salvation. I would like to see Louis' early morning refreshing discipline in the Saint Mary's pool as telling metaphor of his witness to each of us; to be faithful to a daily life of prayer; prayer-in-action.

How are the two combined, so that each makes the other fruitful? There is a formula: "formation through action," which has come to animate us all.

A story may convey it. A few years ago when Louis was suffering from painful arthritis, he decided to go to Brother Andre's Oratory in Montreal and ask that if the Lord wanted him to continue working, he be cured of this illness that was more and more immobilizing him. While in Canada, Louis was given a new drug for arthritis which was not yet available in the USA. He was staying in the Holy Cross house at the Oratory, and had a room at one end of a long, dark corridor with the facilities at the other end (often the case in religious houses!). If he got up during the night, Louis would have to grope his way slowly down that corridor, walking with great pain. One night he got up and was half way down the hall when he suddenly realized that he was walking normally! Once he was telling the story of this recovery, and a community member asked him whether he attributed his cure to Brother Andre or to the new drug. Louis looked at him and said, "Brother Andre would not have asked that question."

Appendix C

Excerpts from Seminary Writings

"The Layman in Seminary Education" from Seminary Education in a time of change, edited by James Michael Lee and Louis J. Putz, C.S.C.

"In the third session of the Council, Pope Paul II emphasized the importance of the layman by appointing to the Council lay consultants. Thus the Council made concrete attempts to restructure the Church in such a radical manner that there will be not only official ecclesiastical recognition for the layman but also that the layman will be able to bring his needs and the solutions to such needs to the immediate attention of the hierarchy. In the future, therefore, the line of demarcation between the teaching Church and the listening Church will not be neatly drawn between cleric and layman as before; rather the line will be drawn within each individual member of the Church. The people of God will then truly be, in the words of Saint Peter, 'a priestly people, a royal priesthood, a holy nation'...

One of the necessary steps toward updating seminary education with respect to a healthy attitude toward the laity is to cultivate in the future priests a profound respect for the layman's primary—but not sole—contribution to the Church. Dedication and/or good will are not enough...

There is a definite necessity of dialogue between seminarian and layman. Such an encounter constitutes an essential start in the formation of clerics. As a personal note, the present writer must remark that during his seminary career it was only through personal experience that he was made aware of the needs of apostolic involvement. This awareness was affected not by his seminary professors but by full-time apostles in the specialized lay movements of Catholic Action, men and women who came periodically to the seminary to speak on the great needs of present-day society. Their testimony was convincing enough to induce the present writer, then a seminarian, to volunteer his help in leading parish groups of J.O.C. in the Communist zone of Paris. He personally owes a great debt to these dedicated lay persons for causing the turning point in his priestly life."

"New Approaches to Seminary Formation," Louis J. Putz, C.S.C.

Reprinted from Ave Maria, *National Catholic Weekly*, May 6, 1967

At Notre Dame's Moreau Seminary we have a team responsible for a certain section of the house: chapel, library, dining room, athletic facilities, inside and outside maintenance. These jobs are assumed by the members of the team under the responsibility of the respective chairmen. Sharing these preoccupations gives the group members a chance to learn to work together as a team, as well as to think together.

At this time the various committees submit to the assembly their findings and plans to be discussed, accepted, rejected or amended, as the case may be. This procedure creates maximum communication and brings about a meeting of the mind of the whole community. It is also a form of educating seminarians to democratic systems.

The lay apostolate is a vital part of formation, and with good guidance the future priest learns to broaden his responsibilities, so necessary to his sense of fulfillment as well ads to his potential for making value judgments and on-the-spot decisions. Seminarians are encouraged to work in the Mexican migrant apostolate: tutoring school-age youngsters, teaching religion, and helping the families to adjust to the environment. Some of our men have been sent to the inner-city areas to gain insights into the racial situation, while others were given an opportunity to work in Mexico, Mississippi, Chicago, Harrisburg, Washington, DC, and Canada, so as to become involved in various social problems. Aside from this summer activity, there is year-round involvement in parish CCD work, assisting Young Christian Students' groups on the grade-school level, and working with the poor, the sick, the blind, the infirm and the mentally retarded.

Saturdays are totally unscheduled except for a Bible Vigil in the evening, which formally introduces the Sunday liturgy. Our Sunday Mass has a special solemnity and significance. We celebrate it at 11 o'clock in the morning, with a homily, music and singing. Among the highlights of the worship is its true community spirit. Students from the University and from St. Mary's College are welcome to participate, as well as the parents of the seminarians, faculty members from the University and their families. This gives the seminarians increased awareness of and training in parish liturgy.

We aim at forming priests who understand the true principle of freedom and authority, priests who can exercise initiative. In an age when all or at least the majority of human beings are educated, the priest is no longer deemed the "sole sage" in the crowd. He must learn to listen to and learn from others who are often better educated than he. Unless he learns to listen while he is being educated, he will never learn to listen after he is ordained. The democratic process of give-and-take must be absorbed early in life. All decision-making need not come from the top down, but many and perhaps the best ideas can come from the ranks. Therefore, the seminary should provide the necessary formation and opportunity for experimentation. If the priest is to be relevant in our modern society, he must learn to listen to the layman about problems he knows better by personal experience.

Appendix D

Eulogy for Louis Putz

Moreau Seminary, June 25th, 1998
David B. Burrell, C.S.C.

Matthew 7:21–29

The gospel acclamation for this morning's portion from Matthew's gospel is taken from John 14:23: "All who love me will keep my words, and my Father will love them, and we will come to them." Together they epitomize Louis's attitude towards scripture, or I should rather say: the import of scripture in his life.

When André called me early on the morning of June 24—the feast of John the Baptist—to say that Louis had died earlier of a massive stroke, I could only respond: "God is good." For Louis would never have managed in a wheelchair! That day a gift was completed, made a total gift by the lord. It is WE who need the stories (and we shall have an opportunity for plenty of them afterwards) to appreciate, collectively, the magnitude, the beauty, the unlikelihood; natively, we prefer to keep it for ourselves! But Louis, and Louis's life, taught us differently; taught us to carpe diem, seize the opportunities for giving, for they come from the Spirit, though it was Louis who often called them to our attention!

How did that gift unfold? That is, how was his response orchestrated so that in the fullness of years, it reached such a symphonic pitch? Many here know the outlines of the story. How his aunt, a Holy Cross sister recruited in the early decades of this century by an enterprising Holy Cross priest, had offered his family this opportunity, and how Louis snatched it up in 1923, in his fourteenth year: how this German-speaking lad attained first in his high school seminary class, complete with the allocution prize, graduating from Notre Dame magna cum laude, and was sent off to France to help re-found Holy Cross there.

How crucially formative were those years, when he was trained in the theology called "new" (nouvelle thélogie) yet which was thoroughly patristic in character—a theology which would be promulgated to the entire church thirty years later in Vatican II, along with the corresponding practice which emphasized the priesthood of all the faithful.

It was that formation which prepared him to bring the fresh air (with which John XXIII later wished to air out the church) to Notre Dame in a harrowing escape from Europe in the dark days of 1940. His early work with students (YCS = Young Christian Students) and young women workers (YCW = Young Christian Workers) began to set the pace, spearheaded by Cannon Cardign's "observe/judge/act" process, animated by the scriptures, and enfleshed in specific actions—usually undermining long-established procedures which had ceased to serve people very well. Using student cadrés formed to an awareness of the import of the gospels, YCS prodded this University to admit people of color, re-cycle books for student use, open avenues of communication and publicity, and revise the residence hall system—all with the over-riding purpose of forming young men and women (for Saint Mary's was an integral part of his work) as "lay apostles," that is, people whose lives radiated the gospel. Cardinal Suhard, the distinguished archbishop of Paris during those times, whose famed pastoral letter, "Growth or Decline?" Louis was later to publish, counseled all Christians to live in such a way that our lives would be incomprehensible without the gospel. In the sixties, this work blossomed into a translation project designed to bring the "new theology" then animating Vatican II into the English-speaking world: Fides Publishers. The impact of this venture proved incalculable, and constituted Louis' venture into the intellectual world which always animated his thinking and acting.

Even Father Kenna, the far-sighted and deep-hearted provincial superior with whom our province was gifted in the transitional sixties, who asked Louis to guide Moreau Seminary into the church which Vatican II envisaged. Characteristically, he sought advice, and published (with James Lee) the ground breaking *Seminary Education in Time of Change*, which proved to be one of the galvanizing lay persons to become church. (Brother Clarence's sister, Sister Judian, recalls how warmly she was welcomed in those years into this milieu.) Only after this immersion in theological education and formation was he prepared to bring the message to "third age" people—first in South Bend, then in Phoenix, Palm Springs, and back to South Bend: Harvest House and the Forever Learning Institute. The rest, as they say, is history. Yet the seeds were sown for a new millennium a church that knows itself to be the people of God. Characteristically, his latest venture, with the Notre

Dame Alumni Association, is titled ND's FIRST: "Fighting Irish Retired Service Team."

At the heart of this diachronic, historical unfolding of a life, is the synchronic, the integrative dimension, where all this comes together to animate each moment of our lives—where the historian gives way to the philosopher! One way of identifying this core secret of a person's life is to attend to what the person sees as its crucial moments or turning points. By Louis' own testimony, the first was a dream of a nine-year old boy, seeing American soldiers on the other side of a river, beckoning him to come with them. He already knew he was not to become a soldier, so this dream sealed his later response on his aunt's offer. Then there were the ten days on Ellis Island at fourteen, where he was interred when the Holy Cross priest assigned to meet his ship was unable to do so. Here, bereft of the language, he met all sorts of people, yet managed to come out safe and sound. This was followed by the aridity of the high school seminary, thankfully alleviated by the German-speaking Holy Cross sisters who worked there and provided a surrogate family for the youngster so recently lifted out of a loving home. Then LeMans and the presence of the great French moral theologian, Jules Lebreton, who lived down the hall and early on recognized Louis' talent. Then there were the postwar student meetings in Vienna, where a miraculous cure of rheumatoid arthritis was accomplished through Brother André's intercession in Montreal in the seventies.

Nor should we fail to mention the setbacks, the disappointments and sadnesses which carve out the places in our hearts for the Spirit to operate. Leaving home and the mother to whom he was so close, denial of the first rank prize at LeMans when Cardinal Grant found out that he was German, the indirect news of his parent's sudden death when an American plane emptied its bomb bay on his village, having missed its primary target. He mentioned now and then his disappointment at never having been asked to do further studies by the Congregation —something which in retrospect would probably have launched him in a direction precluding the kind of flexibility which came to mark his life; and of course recurring lack of support for his ventures and vision of church from hierarchy—tempered by the enthusiastic support of a few bishops. But the last and worst of all, of course, was being told that he could not drive. The reason was purely physical; he had lost some crucial motor control in his left foot, and South Bend stood to gain; but to Louis it meant a relative immobility and having to depend on others— which, of course, he knew very well how to do, but preferred not having to do it!

Finally, to get closer to the secret of his life; his was a vision of faith opened up in his family, articulated in the "new theology" he so avidly absorbed, nourished by prayer and friendship with others. Along with this was a full integration into the vision of Holy Cross: Father Moreau's vision of a community which is a microcosm of church: male and female, lay and clerical. Perfect for him, the "auxiliary priest" image of Holy Cross allows us to serve the church; male and female, lay and clerical puts us at the center of the "people of God." We are not, as Jesuits or Dominicans, a group with a distinguished history; we cannot stand apart: Notre Dame is not a Holy Cross university but a Catholic university, and that inherent modesty well becomes Louis' view of us as a family in the service of God's people.

Funeral Homily for Louis J. Putz, C.S.C.

June 26, 1998

Readings: Romans 8:14–23 and Matthew 25:31–46

Many months ago, Father Putz said to me: "I want you to preach at my funeral." He did not build up to this statement; he simply approached me at Holy Cross House and said it. I said, "Father Putz, I would be honored to preach at your funeral. However, you look in such great health that you could outlive me." He responded, "Good, you will preach at my funeral."

At this point I wanted to add: "Louie, when you were the superior of Moreau Seminary, you sometimes thought that I was Willy Raymond, George Lucas, or Don Fetters. I am Bob Krieg. For your funeral homily, are you sure you're asking the right guy?" I did not pose this question, so it may be that you're about to hear a homily from the wrong person.

I mention my brief conversation with Father Putz because many of you likely had similar encounters with him. That is, it likely happened that he called you and said, "I want you to do something for me. I know that you can do it better than anyone else." You probably responded, "Oh, yes, how can I help?" But you may have simultaneously asked yourself, "Is he asking the right person?" and "How can I say no?"

But there was no saying "No" to Louie Putz. He did not make requests; he gave commands. He had seemingly adopted the speech patterns of God. In the Bible, God said to Abraham and Sarah, "Leave Ur for a new land." Later, Yahweh said to Moses, "Lead my people to freedom." And the angel Gabriel said to Mary, "You will conceive a child and call him Jesus." Finally, Jesus said to his disciples, "Follow me" and "Feed my sheep." Similarly, Louie Putz said to many of us on numerous occasions, "Bring the refreshments" or "Contact everyone in the group" or "Help me raise this money." And each of us said "Okay," even when we did not want to say "Okay."

This commanding, visionary man, Louis J. Putz, C.S.C., had a massive stroke in the early morning hours of Wednesday, June 23, at Holy Cross House and, with Father André Léviellé, C.S.C., and the caring staff of Holy Cross House at his side, he died at 2 a.m. Most of us expected him to live to see his ninetieth birthday next June. True, he was hospitalized earlier this month for a week or so, but it appeared to be a minor problem. Also, he recently spoke about visiting his family in Germany later in the summer. Hence, his sudden death has taken us by surprise. Yet this death fit him. There was no lingering, no half-life. If he could not continue to live vigorously, then he would prefer to die and share in the resurrection of Jesus Christ.

Many years ago, Mrs. Reggie Weissert—who read the first text—foresaw Louie's last days. She said, "Life will not be over for Louie Putz until he turns up his toes and we have a grand wake. Then he will begin a new project." Well, Reggie was right. Louie lived life to the full and then quickly departed for his next mission.

Yet, Louie had lost some of his sparkle over the past two years. He was deeply saddened by the death of his dear friend and close associate Harriet Kroll (a loss that is still felt by her sister Wanda). After Harriet's death, Louie spoke with tears in his eyes when he said that he missed Harriet and that he could not sustain his many service projects without her. In his words, "She's the one who ran everything. We worked together for 50 years. She was wonderful."

So, now Louie will soon catch up with Harriet Kroll and with his many other friends from over the years. And Louie will now begin something new in heaven. I hope that Louie does not shock God.

What has Father Putz left behind? What is his legacy? His lasting gift is twofold: It is his vision of the church and his hope for the church's renewal.

Father Putz envisioned a church in which lay women and lay men—of all ages and with many different gifts and abilities—pooled their talents as they worked for the coming of God's kingdom. In 1993, the South Bend Tribune quoted Louie on our post-Vatican II church: "The church is a new church today. The big emphasis up to now was clerical, but now the church needs to be run by the laity."

Louie made this same point about the church on many occasions when he said that he had pursued a single idea in his many, various projects—namely, that the church includes the laity; indeed, that the laity, along with the clergy, must use their talents for the church's mission. The entire people of God—the clergy and the laity—must give food to the hungry, drink to the thirsty, and shelter to the homeless (Mt. 25).

Father Putz realized this one idea, this theology of the church, in each of his creative endeavors: in the Youth Christian Student Movement (YCS) and in the Christian Family Movement (CFM), which he started with Patty and Pat Crowley and Father Reynold Hillenbrand. He was encouraged in YCS and CFM by Father Theodore Hesburgh, C.S.C., and Monsignor John Egan of Chicago. Also, he made his view of the church concrete in Fides Publishing House and in his many books, especially Seminary Education in a Time of Change (1965). Further, he brought this same ecclesiology to Moreau Seminary, where he served as the superior, and also to the Harvest House movement, the Forever Learning Center, the Family Life Service of the Fort Wayne–South Bend Diocese, and the St. Paul Retirement Community. What an extraordinary list of initiatives and programs! For over sixty years, Louie Putz embodied one prophetic insight in at least nine new forms of life and service.

Of course, Father Putz did not originate this vision of the laity's participation in the church's mission. He adopted it from Canon Joseph Cardijn of Belgium, with whom he worked as a young priest. Further, Putz and Cardijn received this inspired view of the church from St. Paul, who declared that the Holy Spirit calls all people to work for the coming of God's new creation (Rom. 8) and that we must combine our diverse gifts and skills in the building up of the one, living body of Christ (Rom. 12; 1 Cor. 12). Louie Putz's vision of the church was St. Paul's vision of the church. It was also the Second Vatican Council's vision, especially in the documents Lumen Gentium and Gaudium et Spes.

As I conclude, I wish to make a bold comparison; that is, I would like to compare St. Paul and Father Putz. After his conversion, St. Paul dedicated his life to the insight that the Holy Spirit could work among people who were not Jewish. The Council of Jerusalem in AD 49 embraced this revolutionary idea and, as a result, opened the door for the flourishing of the Christian faith among Gentiles. In a similar way, Louie Putz—beginning in the 1930s—gave his life over to the vision that the Holy Spirit calls lay women and lay men to pastoral leadership in the church, along with the priests. Vatican II endorsed this inclusive vision of the church in 1965 and, as a result, set the stage for the blossoming of today's lay ministries.

After their respective church councils, St. Paul and Father Putz matured as men of hope. St. Paul persisted in his missionary work despite many misfortunes. Louie Putz relentlessly pursued his vision for sixty years. Since Vatican II, some Catholics have become anxious about the church's future. Not Father Putz. He did not fret about the number of seminarians or about changes in church structures. Rather, he was enthusiastic about the seminarians in the Congregation of Holy Cross and also about the emergence of the laity's new roles in parish life as they work beside their priests. Moreover, he continued to hope that the Holy Spirit would bring about the church's renewal.

Many years ago, Mrs. Reggie Weissert observed that life would not be over for Louie Putz until he had turned up his toes, after which he would begin new projects in heaven. May Father Louis J. Putz, C.S.C., now start his new mission in paradise, and may we at this Eucharist give thanks to God for the life of this hope-filled visionary.

Louie, we bid you farewell. We will miss you. Yet, we know that, among the saints, you will pray for us and our renewal in the Holy Spirit. Finally, we promise you that we will sustain your vision—the vision of the Second Vatican Council—into the new millennium.

Robert A. Krieg, C.S.C.
Theology Department
Notre Dame, Indiana 46556-5639

Appendix E

Father Putz Homilies

Introduction to Part II

What follows are homilies from Fr. Putz. You are encouraged to read them on a regular basis and to reflect on them as an individual or in a group of friends. Then ask what current situation in today's society do they shed light on? Then consider what action might be appropriate and finally ask the question how did the action go? How could it be better next time? As the title says, "You are Church!"

Homilies

Prayer and Brotherhood

The two are intimately connected. Without prayer, there will never be any true brotherhood. We are brought face to face with the paradox of Christianity. Jesus came to feed the hungry, to give drink to the thirsty, to clothe the naked, to give shelter to the homeless, to offer peace to a war-torn world, to raise the dead to life. As a matter of fact, He did all these things. He pardoned the sinner, He fed the four thousand, He cured the blind man, and He raised the dead son of the widow mother, the daughter of Jairus, the friend Lazarus from the dead.

Yet, He did not do away with disease, He did not do away with hunger, He did not do away with war. The four horsemen are riding the highways and byways of the world more savagely than ever. Has Christianity failed?

Christianity has not failed. It has not been tried. Brotherhood cannot be achieved without prayer. Prayer is the act of humility, the act of faith which declares itself unable to love without the help of God. When we love with our own puny efforts, then there is going to be disappointment.

Consider the wedding couple of Cana. They threw a banquet. They had pooled their resources but soon they were to be disappointed. The whisper went all around, they have no wine. What an embarrassment. The acknowledgement of their predicament was their salvation. Jesus came to the rescue magnificently. They have more wine, better wine than ever. This is Christ's response to their prayer.

Martha and Mary had a sick brother. They sent a delegation. Our brother is sick. Christ waits, He tarries, and the brother dies. What a pity, what sorrow. Had He been here he would not have died. The prayer of hope, the prayer of inadequacy, will be richly answered. He will rise again, even on the last day, forever.

Until we acknowledge our poverty, our inability to cope with our needs, until we depend on God through prayer to come to the rescue, there will not be genuine brotherhood; there will not be genuine love. What is lacking to our love is precisely the universality that only God gives, the totality of love that Jesus gave, the love that does not count the cost.

Only God knows our people as they are. Only God can give a total love. To love without expecting a return on our love, this is divine love.

Only this kind of love will save the world.

Incarnation, Christ becoming one of us, is the great paradox of Christianity. Christ has risen, but He wants to rise in each one of us. When this happens because we seek Him, then we can count on Christianity succeeding. The world will rise to a new life, to a new love, to a new resurrection—in each one of us. Without prayer, without prayer that unites, there is no brotherhood. Let us lead the way to a new life in Christ, to recognizing Him in our brother. Let us offer not merely a human love, but a divine love with the enrichment that comes of communing in the love of Christ.

Thanksgiving

On the day of Thanksgiving, we still do not have a Mass proper for Thanksgiving Day. I want to use Mary's hymn of thanksgiving as a framework of my little homily.

Let us in the spirit of Mary, the spirit of the Magnificat, praise God for all the many favors He has granted us during this year.

"My soul magnifies the Lord and my spirit rejoices in God my Savior."

Like Mary, we have cause for great joy and thanksgiving. God is using us – He needs us to accomplish His work. This is cause for great joy. Without our help, God cannot bring about the miracle of growth that He intends to effect in each one of us: We want to grow up, to become good students, good candidates for the priesthood, for the religious life, good Christians above all. This is all what God wants to accomplish in us and through us but not without us. He has given us this tremendous opportunity to be co-helpers with God in the work of our own salvation, our own maturing process.

Let us thank God for this.

"Because He has regarded the lowliness of his handmaid, for behold all generations shall call me blessed."

St. Paul: "Gladly I will glory in my infirmities that the strength of Christ may dwell in me. Wherefore I am satisfied, for Christ's sake with infirmities, with insults, with hardships, with persecutions, with distresses. For when I am weak, then I am strong."

We can say the same thing. God fulfills his plan through imperfect means. Which one of us can say that we have been always completely faithful, completely honest, completely truthful, completely dedicated, and yet, God was able to use us and He relies on us to do His work. He accepts us for what we are, feeble, now good, now mediocre, now bad, but He is still on our side and bringing good out of evil, good out of mediocre people. Let us thank God for His confidence, His love.

"He hath shown might in his arm, He has scattered the proud in the conceit of their heart."

Mary, and we with Mary, rejoice to see the expansion of the kingdom of God. We see the mustard seed in us grow into a tree which is capable of bearing fruit, sometimes decently good fruit. The important thing to realize is that God confided His most important work, the establishment of the kingdom of God into human hands, our hands. This is something to realize whether it is being parents of children, or being in charge of our community, being in charge of apostolates, but we are in charge of the kingdom of God which is both within us and outside us.

The kingdom of God suffereth violence and it is the violent that bear it away. Who are the violent? They are those who mean business, who are anxious to work and to perform the work God has assigned them.

"He has put the mighty from their thrones and has exalted the lowly."

Again, the Lord knows how to reverse the normal situation. Look at the world's mighty and powerful of yesterday. Where are they today? Who admires a Hitler, a Stalin, a Mussolini? God brought them to their downfall. But God knows how to bring good out of little people like ourselves. At God's judgment seat we shall know who is preferred by God. Let us thank God for our littleness so that He can bring good from little people.

"He has filled the hungry with good things and the rich He has sent away empty."

There is so much we can be thankful for today. Let us consider that two-thirds of the people in this world are hungry, physically hungry, and under those conditions they cannot do their best work. Yet there is not too much hunger in our lives. Maybe there are hungry people in our midst but we have enough to be satisfied. Our Thanksgiving goes to God for making us part of America which is blessed beyond all measure compared to the rest of the hungry world. Let us be thankful.

"He has given help to Israel, his servant, mindful of his misery."

God is good to all people, to all nations and we should rejoice when this happens. We must not be selfish, clutching to our own wealth, our own security. We must be big and generous with our God-given goods. Let us be grateful for all the charitable enterprises of our friends, of our society and community, of our nation, of the United Nations. This is all to the good.

"Even as he spoke to our fathers, to Abraham and to his posterity forever."

God is faithful to his promises. He will not disappoint us. If we are faithful in this time, in this life, He will reward us a thirty fold, sixty fold, a hundred fold according to our own generosity. To be with God, to be with Love Eternal, is the great goal of life, the sum total of all that is good and desirable. Let us aspire to it. God is good.

Lourdes

February 10, 1942

Next Wednesday, the Church will be commemorating the Feast of the Apparitions of the Blessed Virgin to Bernadette at Lourdes. For most of you, the story of the apparitions is a very familiar one; you are reviewing it every time you pay your visit to the Grotto, a replica of that at Lourdes. Briefly, the story is this: On 18 different occasions in 1858 – 4 years after the solemn declaration of the dogma of the Blessed Virgin Mary – the Virgin Mary appeared to a 14-year old peasant girl in a town of the Pyrenees. Since that time, her shrine has achieved a world fame equaled by no other. Thousands of people of all social conditions and all nationalities visit it annually to pay their respects and to submit their petitions to the Virgin of Lourdes. Moreover, replicas of the famous grotto have been erected in every corner of the globe where the loyal children of the Mother of God receive solace from their heavenly patroness.

In view of this astonishing fact, we may justly ask ourselves the reason, the Why, of all this fame and this unaccountable reputation. There have been many appearances of the Blessed Virgin and many other places have been so favored. Just what does Lourdes signify to justify its unique place in the esteem of Christians the world over? God must have had some design in commissioning His Mother to show her power at Lourdes. And if we stop briefly to consider the particular evils and errors of our times, we find the clue to the solution of this problem.

The nineteenth and twentieth centuries especially have been worshippers of Man and of his prowess in the scientific field, believers in the Gospel of unlimited material progress. Lourdes is God's challenge to this idolatry. The modern world has made comfort and painless processes a beatitude; Lourdes is God's answer to the modern desire to escape from pain and suffering. Peace treaties, disarmament conferences, and humanitarian idealism have failed miserably to establish order among nations; Lourdes is God's solution to the problem of international peace.

First of all, Lourdes is God's answer to the Agnostic and Pseudo-Scientific cult of man and nature. (I say Pseudo-Scientist, because the real scientist understands not only the possibilities of his field, but also its limitations.) Around the middle of the last century it became very fashionable to reject all belief in the supernatural, in miracles, in a God-created, God-controlled world. The Liberalist, the progressive mind of the day, considered himself free to believe what he liked; but he was especially inclined to disbelieve everything that he could not see with his own eyes, touch with his own hands, or prove with his own arguments. The doctor's scalpel finds no trace of a soul in the human body; therefore, there is no soul. Christ talked unscientific language; therefore, Christ was a fake. A miracle escapes the range of vision of the microscope; therefore, miracles are impossible and must be explained away as illusions or hysteria. Evolution and human inventiveness alone hold out infinite possibilities, infinite hopes – infinite progress. So believed the fashionable mind of that day!

Lourdes shattered this worshipful scientism. Again, as in the Gospel text, Christ brought out a child to lead them – the doctors and the scribes: "Unless you become as one of these, you shall not enter into the Kingdom of heaven." An illiterate girl of fourteen was chosen to carry God's message to a world of unbelievers. Bernadette Soubirous – a frail, asthmatic child of very poor circumstances, with no dreams of or desire for international fame – became the confidante of the Virgin Immaculate. The instructions were few, but bold. A shrine was to be erected and pilgrimages organized. Each successive visit was pre-arranged; and people – both curious and faithful – swarmed into the place if not to see the vision, at least to see its marvelous effects on Bernadette herself.

But toward the end, it became evident that the visions were not intended primarily for her. Our Lady appeared in this recess of the mountain to speak to the entire world – to bring it to its knees, to urge it to penance and humility to a recognition of the rights of God. "I am the Immaculate Conception," she gratefully and humbly proclaimed herself; and with the zeal of the Mother of God, things began to happen. Cures were reported; the newly discovered spring was declared to have miraculous healing qualities; more and more people were attracted; the crowds had to be housed or turned away. Almost reluctantly the ecclesiastical authorities had to sanction the event and to approve the irresistible throng of pilgrims, until lately in normal times, several regional and national pilgrimages crowd the streets of Lourdes and the avenues leading to the Shrine every day. Two basilicas have been built, and even these are insufficient to accommodate even the more moderately sized pilgrimages.

These are material realizations that only a supernatural, miraculous origin can explain. Far more important is the constant trek of intellectuals – believers and unbelievers – to the Lady's shrine, where often they find their lost faith or discover its light for the first time. Lourdes attracts everyone and captivates even the unbeliever; for there he is definitely within the reach of the supernatural. Lourdes is a veritable city of faith; you breathe it – radiate it – manifest it in the most childlike manner. For there, in the home of our Mother, there is no human respect.

Secondly, Lourdes is God's challenge to the modern stress on ease and comfort. The emphasis of the man of today is definitely toward a philosophy of the material paradise. There are manifold appeals to the senses: overstuffed furniture, soft garments, expensive foods, nightclub psychology – the conspicuous consumption of the leisure class – luxurious living – the artificial stimulation of sensual appetites. And characteristic of the average man of today are such tendencies as the flight from pain and work, the desire for a quick and sure relief from the least discomfiture, the shirking of responsibilities (especially along intellectual lines), the shunning of suffering as the supreme evil, the everlasting search for security, for pleasure, for a surcease from duty. You will notice these traits in the lives of your fellow students – and perhaps in your own. It is a philosophy that puts the supreme value on the things of the flesh, not on the things of the spirit.

Lourdes is definitely a challenge to this mentality. Of the thousands who go to Lourdes to be cured, very few are actually freed from their infirmities. But they go back home with a new life and a new hope: they have discovered the value of suffering. How often it happens that a sick person at the sight of many more sick than himself will ask Our Lady to let him keep his affliction and to cure the others. On the days of the great pilgrimages, Lourdes is a veritable ocean of human misery; yet on no face will you discover despair – not even the most mutilated, the most hopeless cases. The sick are plunged into a cold bath till the water, which is changed only once every day, is putrid with filth. Many there will drink that water; yet no one has ever been heard to have contracted a disease at Lourdes, nor has any epidemic ever shown itself, despite the presence of all manner of contagious disease.

During one of her apparitions, Our Lady solemnly warned the world to get on its knees; three times she called out, "Penance, Penance, Penance!" Not the lack of good things, but too much of them was destroying the human race. We need to appreciate again the value of a mortified and ascetical life. We must learn to dominate the cravings of the appetites in order to better attend to the things of the spirit. St. Bernadette herself is an example. While Our Lady was curing people at Lourdes, she was dying of a lingering illness – a young, but broken body. The Blessed Virgin had promised her happiness, but not in this life. Lourdes seems to emphasize again that man is made to earn his bread by the sweat of his brow – and his salvation through the Cross.

Finally, Lourdes is God's answer to the problem of international peace. Many praiseworthy attempts have been made to establish peace among nations, peace among classes, peace among races. All attempts have come to naught in what seems now to be an ever-increasing madness and chaos. Lourdes holds the solution: mutual understanding through reciprocal love and service in the home of the common Mother of redeemed mankind. Men and women of all nationalities come to Lourdes. There they pray in their own tongue to the same Father of all; they rub elbows with pilgrims from Germany or England, Spain or Scandinavia, America or Asia. At Lourdes, all men are brothers; and you will see eminent men of letters or doctors or lawyers serving as stretcher-bearers for black or white, rich or poor, Greek or barbarian. Lourdes is an object lesson in the only possible way peace can ever be established among the peoples: they must adore and love the same God as their Father, venerate the same Immaculate Virgin as their Mother; then only will they see in their neighbor – whoever he may be – their brother.

I need not urge you, dear students, to faith – and hope – and charity. I need not convince you of the necessity of penance. I'll ask you only to learn to love the Grotto while you are here at Notre Dame and to bear that love away with you. The Grotto and the Immaculate One whom it manifests will impart to you the lessons that made Lourdes a new mercy of God to the world.

Christ Our Brother

"Blessed are your eyes, because they see, and your ears because they hear. For verily I say unto you many prophets and just men have desired to see the things that you see and hear the things that you hear and have not heard them." -St. Matthew

"God who, at sundry times and in diverse manners, spoke in times past to the fathers by the prophets, last of all in these days hath spoken to us by His Son." (Hebrews I, 1)

To the chosen people God had manifested Himself in several striking ways: to Moses the Lord spoke from a burning bush; He led the Israelites through the desert in a column of light and He proclaimed His law to them from trembling, quaking Mount Sinai. Marvelous interventions when one considers that at the same time the pagan world had been left to its own lights. But God had still greater favors in store for man and this is not destined for one nation only but to all men of good will. "As many as would receive Him," says Saint John, "He gave them power to be made the Sons of God." To make us children of God, He had first to become our Brother, our equal; to raise us up to Him, to bring us near Him; he stooped down to us, becoming an infant in swaddling clothes. "His name would be Emmanuel," Isaiah had predicted, that is to say, "God with us."

What a tremendous turning point in man's relationship with God; what a tremendous event for all of humanity; yet none but Mary knew of the coming of Christ. Only a few shepherds and three mysterious kings from the Orient were secretly summoned to the stable of Bethlehem. There had been a good deal more stir at the birth of John the Baptist, as Saint Luke records: "All things relating to John's birth were noised abroad over all the hill country of Judea." No such publicity for our Savior. The topsy-turvy world, with all its craving for news and latest reports missed the greatest of all events, the birth of its God, its King. The few visits at Bethlehem did not disturb the society of the day any more than the slight breeze would ripple an agitated ocean.

The story of Bethlehem, dear friends, is the story of the tabernacle. The manger was the first monstrance. The same Babe, the son of Mary, whom the Magi had come so far to see and to adore, is present here under the appearance of a white host. There was nothing kingly or even divine about the Babe on his straw bed, or in Mary's arms, but the whole scene did appear very brotherly. For Christ is our Brother indeed, for that He came into the world, to make us by His redeeming death children of God and if we are children of God His Father then we are brothers to Christ. After the resurrection, Our Lord appeared to Mary Magdalene and he told her, "Go to my brethren, and say to them I ascend to my Father and to your Father, to my God and to your God." And Saint Paul writes to the Hebrews: "For both he that sanctifieth, and they who are sanctified, are all of one. For which cause he is not ashamed call them brethren," and the same apostle calls Christ the first-born among many brethren. Christ, therefore, is our older brother and we his little brothers and to be sure He feels all the tenderness and all the self-sacrificing devotedness that a big brother feels for his younger brothers. And to think that this older brother is the all power-ful God Himself with all the riches and forces of heaven and earth at His command, to think that He is just as much of a man as we are with a heart that feels and thinks like ours, that understands the misery and weakness, but also the infinite aspirations of the human heart, to think that this older brother of ours is here present on the altar, that He remains here under the same roof with us day and night awaiting our confidences, wishing to share our trials and sufferings as well as our joys is simple, powerful truth and should inspire us with a great confidence for our holy faith on that is the occasion of so many and so great favors; but at the same time, dear friends, this thought of Christ's intimate life and companionship with us should provoke a very serious and practical question in our minds: What is our behavior towards Him in our daily life? Do we treat Him as our Brother? Or is He a mere stranger to us? In short, have we discovered Christ?

That is the very lesson that tomorrow's feast should bring home to us. The Magi had discovered Christ because with the help of God they took pains to find Him. Let us follow the inspired text: "When Jesus therefore was born in Bethlehem of Judea, in the days of King Herod, behold, there came wise men from the east to Jerusalem, saying Where is he that is born King of the Jews? For we have seen his star in the east and are come to adore him. And King Herod hearing this, was troubled and all Jerusalem with him." Three simple hearted, God fearing wise men, pagans at that, had seen a star, the call of God and following the voice of their conscience they did not hesitate to undertake a perilous, fatiguing, and uncertain journey through desert land to pay their hom-age to the new born King. And coming to Jerusalem naturally enough they expected to find Him in the royal palace. "And King Herod hearing this, was troubled and all Jerusalem with him," adds the sacred writer. To think that the Jews, the chosen people, whom God had entrusted with the sacred books, who knew where the Messiahs would be found, would not so much as take the trouble to look him up too busy as they were with their worldly occupations, whereas, the wise men not in the least discouraged set out anew and their faith was plentifully rewarded for when they had left Jerusalem the star reappeared. "And seeing the star they rejoiced with exceeding great joy. "And entering into the house," continues Saint Matthew, "they found the child with Mary his mother, and falling down they adored him." Although from the mere human point of view the wise men might have been disappointed finding an infant devoid of all that kings call their due; yet they had the faith and the poor surroundings did not prevent them from seeing God in the infant in Mary's arms, "and opening their treasures, they offered him gifts: gold, frankincense and myrrh."

The three wise men had discovered Christ, but at the cost of a painstaking search. Like them, we are called to go after Christ; our religious vocation is our guiding star. But being called does not mean having arrived. Many days of weary journeying, cloudy days and starless nights will beset our way, but if we do not let ourselves be deceived or beguiled by the dazzle and glamour of the world, Herod's court, and discouraged by the indifference of our associates, then we can be sure that we too shall discover Christ. Let this word not surprise you, dear friends, we will discover Christ, for we must grow daily in the knowledge of God in order to love and serve Him better. This is the pearl of great price for which we should be ready to sacrifice everything; this is the buried treasure that is worth a whole life's efforts to discover.

Now let us depose tonight at the feet of the Eucharistic crib the gold of our charity, divine and fraternal, the frankincense of our prayers and adoration, the myrrh of our mortified life and let us humbly ask in return a deeper faith, a more perfect understanding, a greater appreciation of the gift of God in the Holy Eucharist. Wherever we find Jesus, we alike find His Mother. She, who was His interpreter with the shepherds and the wise men, is ever ready to teach us her science of faith, her language of love, and her secrets for the service of Her Son.

Sermon of Zeal

The subject for this Sunday's instruction is the virtue of zeal. A most fitting topic, you will agree, on the day of Pentecost, on the day on which the divine fire of zeal bolted like a hurricane from the throne of God into the hearts of men. Aflame with that sacred fire and with our Lord's last command, "Go teach all nations," still ringing in their ears, the small group of Apostles burst open the doors of the Cenacle with an energetic resolve to tell the world of Christ, of Him who was come to save the world.

On the first Pentecost, the Church chalked up an enrollment of three thousand converts; these, in turn, carried their faith with enthusiasm to the four corners of the earth. From small beginnings, the Catholic Church rose and developed into a numerous family, as the Christian leaven slowly but irresistibly worked its way into the marrow of society, into the masses of the great Roman Empire. Peter and Paul were zealous men, but even they would have accomplished little had it not been for the help they received from Appollo, from Prisca and Aquilla, and a host of other laymen and women who put their time and their talents into the balance for Christ. Thus, within a relatively short time the great Roman family of nations was changed from a pagan into a Christian commonwealth.

Today we seem to be far from the enthusiasm of the early days of the Church. The world is again on the offensive. Worldly standards are preached from the housetop by radio, press and cinema, are endangering not only public morality but the individual's faith. Even the Catholic home and school influence seems incapable to stop the pagan flood. Hence, with every passing day the Pope calls out more entreatingly for Catholic lay help, Catholic lay apostolate. The world will be saved says Pius XI, only if the layman awakes fully to his responsibilities in the Church, the responsibilities of a fighting soldier in Christ's army. By Baptism you are incorporated as an active cell into the mystical Body of Christ with a special function to fulfill where no one else can replace you, just as in the human organism every cell, every organ, every member has a proper function all of its own. By Confirmation you are called to a more active participation in the spiritual offensive against pagan forces; by your college education you are destined for Catholic leadership with all that leadership implies: knowledge of your faith, zeal in defending it and in spreading it. You are in duty bound to exercise this apostolate later as a Catholic doctor, or a businessman or a lawyer. There is no better way to know the trade than to practice it. As a student, your field of apostolate is the campus, your fellow student.

I can read an objection in your eyes. There is no need for the apostolate here with all the priests and all the religious atmosphere that pervades this campus. Yet there is need for it. In the classroom, on the playground, in the field house, in your hall, everywhere you have your neighbor, your pal or fellow student. You know him better than anyone else; you know his problems, his difficulties, his needs, his aspirations.

But how can I become a good influence in my neighbor's life without boring him to death? By acts of kindness, by timely advice, by services rendered. Too often we pose ourselves as saviors of the world by philosophical, if not sophisticated, theorizing from an armchair; and all the while we evade our responsibilities in the concrete. We talk about peace and war in Europe, but refuse to stifle the smarting retort to someone we dislike; we vehemently discuss communism and its dangers but selfishly squander our dimes and quarters on trifles when so many of God's poor are in dire need of the necessary; we insist violently on our rights while we flagrantly disregard those of our roommate or next door neighbor. If brotherly neighborly charity is the thermometer of our Love for God, how far is it from the freezing point? Ought it not to reach the boiling point?

The Christians of the early Church should serve as our models. What was the secret of their success? The answer lies in the sincerity with which they translate the Gospel into their daily life. They were not mere believers, but actors, missionaries, missionaries to their immediate neighborhood. Thus, the slave of the mines converted his fellow slave, the toga-ed Roman worked on his friend of the Forum, and the Roman lady treated her army of slaves as brothers and sisters. "Who among the pagans," asks Tertullian, "would permit his wife to walk through distant streets and to enter the poorest dwellings to visit the brethren? Who would permit them to enter secretly into dungeons for the purpose of kissing the chains of the martyrs? Or participate in eating and drinking, to beg for food for the poor?" This portrayal of the Roman lady's apostolate comes from the pen of an eyewitness; proud Romans though they were and conquerors of the world, they humbly performed their Christian apostolate that so astounded the pagans, to cause them to exclaim in sheer admiration; "See how they love one another!"

Charity, real effective, personal charity was the wellspring of the zeal of the early Christians. They loved all men because all are children of the one common Father, who makes the sun shine upon good and bad alike; they loved all men because all were saved in the Blood of their elder Brother, Jesus Christ. "Whatever you do to the least of these my brethren, you shall have done it unto me." No idle phrasing here. With the poor they shared their wealth, with the suffering their sympathy, with the slave and the social outcast their meals and interest. "All were of one mind and soul," says Saint Luke, "nor was there any needy among them". No selfish clutch on their wealth for the sake of a certain standard of living or social prestige. Like a mighty flood, their charity destroyed class barriers and leveled social distinctions. The Christian love of neighbor was the secret of their apostolate, the wellspring of their zeal.

Charity, we know, is self-diffusive; charity is good, is patient, is not arrogant, is not repulsing. Charity, personal charity, is the master key that will open every heart. Here is a field for an apostolate that lies at everybody's door. You need not be a powerful speaker to practice neighborly, Christian love; you need not even go out of your way to find an occasion for it. You need neither wealth nor position. On the Day of Reckoning, Christ's sentence will not bear on your assistance at Mass nor on your fasts and abstinence (these are means to an end), nor will good intentions be of any avail, but it will call for your concrete acts of love: "I was hungry and you gave me to eat; I was thirsty and you gave me to drink; I was a stranger and you took me in; naked and you covered me; sick and in prison and you visited me." Why does Christ put such a high value, such heavy stakes, upon the Works of Mercy that here He makes them the great test on which we are judged in that final examination? Saint John provides the answer: "If any man say, I love God, and hateth his brother, he is a liar. For He that loveth not his brother, whom he seeth, how can he love God whom he seeth not?"

These two great realities: the Fatherhood of God and the Brotherhood of Christ should fill us with a deep sense of our dignity, but also with a keen insight into our responsibilities. Can we afford to see our fellow student lose his soul or even jeopardize his salvation without ourselves being stirred to the depths of our hearts with the desire to help and to restore the prodigal to our Father's embrace? Can we remain indifferent when so many even of our immediate relations and friends do not possess the supernatural helps that the sacraments provide to the members of the one true Church, and not burn with a holy zeal until we shall have brought them into the one fold of the true Shepherd? Pious ravings, some will object: am I to importune my friends and become a bore and a killjoy or perhaps a laughingstock? Strange disciple of Christ this one would make who sets human considerations before eternal values: More over, will not true zeal devise a hundred and one ways of attacking without ever becoming a pest? Prayers, sacrifices, and above all acts of kindness and charity—all done perseveringly and tenaciously? I do not think that Christ can refuse you such a conquest that is all to His honor and glory.

In conclusion, let us ask the Holy Spirit on this Day of Pentecost to grant us a spark of that divine fire that so transformed the Chosen Twelve from a timid, fearful fisher-folk into staunch defenders and zealous propagators of God's kingdom on earth. No dreary, forlorn life that of the apostle, but a life that fully satisfies because it spends itself not on trifles, but for God.

Today the world sets before our eyes a beautiful specimen of zeal, the pure, limpid, disinterested, self-sacrificing zeal of the Mother. She it is who makes the poorest home a paradise by her winning ways, her delicate manners, her tender concern for everyone, her sweet smile, in one word: her love. While thanking God for so great a favor, a Christian Mother, while asking Him to bless and protect her in every way, let us learn a lesson from her, and let us acquire the motherly touch in winning souls to Christ.

The Power of Good Example

In last week's *Sunday Visitor*, in the Youth Section, you may have noticed the letter of Jim, a non-Catholic aviator writing to his Catholic friend in St. Louis. The letter mentions an incident that happened in a makeshift hospital somewhere in Australia. That incident changed the life of this non-Catholic who subsequently became a Catholic and would have become a priest had not his life come to a sudden end on the 24th of last March. I quote:

There was a boy in the bed next to me, did I say boy? He hardly could be called that now, both legs and one arm had been blown off, and God: what was left of his face, I'll never forget. Those great dark pain filled eyes will haunt me the rest of my life. A priest, small of stature, came in to administer the last rites to him and those eyes took on a heavenly light, pain seemed to be forgotten in those sacred moments. You know I have never been a religious man, but I felt the presence of a power much greater than all the devils of war. That holy little priest held in his hand what seemed to be a small round disk, but I felt there was something beyond the human understanding in that small round wafer for the boy's eyes rested upon it for a moment, then closed. I saw the priest bend over him, then say a few hurried prayers. The boy had looked at his God through a veil of mystery but when he opened his eyes again the veil was lifted for he was face to face with God. How beautiful to die like that! If I live to be a hundred I'll never forget that scene.

Signed, Jim

Well, Jim never lived to be a hundred. Because of his injuries he was released from the Service and was returned to the States. A priest gave him instructions and received him into the Church. The FBI reemployed him. Then, on a difficult case last spring in New York, Jim was critically shot. He died in less than a week.

After the grace of God, it was the Faith of the boy shining through those dark pain-filled eyes that provided the occasion for this non-Catholic's conversion. Neither the boy nor the priest were probably aware that their actions were being so closely observed. They were simply about their Father's business. But it is precisely when we are about our Father's business, God's business of putting first things first that we are the shining light that we are called to be for those unhappy ones who have not yet found the pearl of great price, divine grace, the life of God in the soul.

The power of example, dear students, the power of a true Christian life is something tremendous. By instinct and social nature we are hero worshippers. The freckled red-haired eighth grader worships his hero of the gridiron. The young man or woman has their favorite movie star. The grown man has his political, military, or business idol. The Church, too, presents us daily with some outstanding examples of a successful career in the pursuit of sanctity. It goes to prove that we like to see our ideal become flesh and blood. We want our ideal incarnate. What use is a word, were it even the divine Word, if it were nothing more than a word, an abstract idea? Man always feels the need of seeing, touching, hearing; and he does not allow himself to be easily won by an idea which is nothing else than an idea. A word by itself has rarely any motive power, it's rarely dynamic. Let an officer show his men the written order received from a higher officer, that they are to "go over the top," to go and meet death. The men will not budge. But let him advance at the head of his company; then the men will follow.

God Himself recognized this human tendency to follow a living ideal of flesh and blood. He was not satisfied to give us His revelation in a book. He sent His divine Word in human flesh. "And the Word was made flesh and dwelt amongst us." He came to do and to teach. First He came to do, then to teach. "Take up your cross," he said, "and come follow Me." If Christ had called us to the practice of poverty solely by His teaching in the sermon of the Mount, "Blessed are the poor," if He had lived the life of a prince, then few men would have sought their happiness in poverty. But Christ lived as a poor man. He was born poor; he died poor. This makes it easier to follow Him. Take, for example, in our day and age the tremendous moral force of a Mahatma Gandhi, the leader of Indian freedom; the example of his frugal penitential life is putting our bourgeois civilization to shame. It is the secret weapon that defies prison walls and armies.

Child psychologists tell us that children learn principally by imitating others. Children are quick to detect inconsistencies. The saying, "Monkey see, monkey do" usually applied to children, is a very true observation of human conduct. How many people have we kept from studying as a sacred duty and obligation? How many did we influence to do a dishonest job, cribbing for example? How many were led to disorderly habits of reading, of dating, of conversation by our example? In this matter we cannot shake off our responsibility. We are our brother's keeper. How many have we kept from reaching the light of faith by our non-Catholic conduct? Many a non-Catholic student, for instance, has said: "I would like to be a Catholic when I see some of these fellows around here – the best boys I ever saw. But I wouldn't want to be a hypocrite, like some of the others."

Here is Student A whose conversion was retarded five years because one day he reminded a Catholic student in Lyons Hall that it was Friday. The Catholic replied: "Meat tastes as good to me on Friday as any other day," and he finished his sandwich.

Student B used to get his Catholic fellow students into arguments in defense of their faith, and when the argument got strong enough he would say: "Well, if I believed what you say you believe, I wouldn't act as you do." B is still an agnostic.

Student C stated: "I go to prayers more faithfully than any Catholic student I know; I don't use the language they use, and I certainly wouldn't do the things some of them say they do. Why should I be a Catholic?" C is still a non-Catholic.

God holds us responsible not only for our personal conduct but for the influence that our conduct might have upon our fellow men. We cannot elbow our way into heaven. We must take our neighbors along with us. This is so true that on the Day of Judgment, Christ will judge us on that criterion. "Because you did it to the least of my brethren, you did it unto Me, enter into the joy of the Lord..." "Because you did not do it to the least of my brethren, you did it not to Me; depart from Me ye cursed..."

The best way of meriting the favorable sentence for the lips of Our Lord, the best way of making sure that we are giving good example at all times, it to take a positive militant part in our religious life. We must not only aim to do good, but become apostles of our environment, centers of life and radiation. How can we become apostles? We can become apostles by analyzing carefully and systematically our influence on our environment, by studying the wants and needs of our fellow students and fulfilling those needs to the best of our ability. What would Christ do on the campus of Notre Dame as one of the students? He would undoubtedly help a poor fellow in his studies without being solicited. He would be quick and sensitive to another's loneliness and homesickness. He would offer sympathy and encouragement to those dejected by bad news from home or failure in exam. He would be seen as one of the boys, afflicted with the same problems as all the others, but always willing and ready to pitch in wherever help was needed. Above all, He would make the best of His studies and student life; He would make it His Father's business.

You see, dear students, it is not merely a matter of giving good example here or there, of impressing others with superior virtue, but it is a matter of living such a full and rich and joyous life that others cannot escape the influence of our presence. In that way, and in that way only, we shall all have the same unearthly gleam in our eyes as the boy of Jim's letter had as He entered into the joy of the Lord. That is my dearest wish for every one of you. Please God that you all become apostles, lay apostles, working your heads off for Christ and His Holy Church in the persons of your fellow students.

Restoring All Things in Christ

In this short sentence, the subject of today's instruction, St. Paul packed all the life of the Christian. In this short sentence, we have also the formula of a world revolution. Did you ever ask yourself seriously what this Christian life is all about? Don't we take it too much for granted without giving it even much thought?

One day, it was a very hot day, Christ stopped at a roadside fountain to rest. He was thirsty for it was the noon hour. As he sat there, a woman approached to draw water. Jesus said to her, "Give me to drink." Taken aback by the request, she said, "How is it that thou, although a Jew, dost ask drink of me, who am a Samaritan woman?" We know that Jews and Samaritans were not on speaking terms. With the woman's curiosity aroused, Jesus immediately takes the conversation to higher levels: He said to her, "If thou didst know the gift of God, and who it is who says to thee, 'Give me to drink,' thou, perhaps, wouldst have asked of him, and he would have given thee living water." The woman said to him, "Sir, thou hast nothing to draw with and the well is deep. Whence then hast thou living water? Art thou greater than our father Jacob who gave us the well, and drank from it, himself, and his sons, and his flocks?" In answer Jesus said to her, "Every one who drinks of this water will thirst again. He, however, who drinks of the water that I will give him shall never thirst; but the water that I will give him shall become in him a fountain of water, springing up unto life everlasting." The woman said to him, "Sir, give me this water that I may not thirst or come here to draw."

Of what water is in question here? There are of two sorts. The one that quenches the thirst, but only for a time; whoever drinks of this water will thirst again; this water the Samaritan woman came to draw everyday. It came from natural sources. The other water of which Christ speaks quenches the thirst once and for all. "He who drinks of the water that I shall give shall never thirst; this water shall become in him a fountain of water, springing up unto life everlasting." This wonderful water is the supernatural life—the life of Christ in our souls and bodies. All the riches and beauties of earth, both spiritual and material, this gift of God overreaches. Whatever these goods might be: be they honors, riches, pleasures, natural qualities of body, mind or heart, health, beauty, knowledge, eloquence, ability of all kinds, genius, heroism, all this without the state of grace, without the life-giving supernatural water, is nothing but dross and vanity, possibly fuel for the eternal fire. God frequently leaves these to his enemies. How is it that the devil is so intelligent and yet so vile? Because in the eyes of God, the natural without the supernatural has only an earthly value, and ephemeral character.

Too many of us have a very faulty and negative view of the supernatural. The supernatural for some of us is nothing but a litany of dos and don'ts, of religious practices without much wit or meaning. Sunday observance, Friday abstinence, Novena devotions, Ten Commandments of God, and so many more commandments of the Church limit the Catholic's freedom. Secretly, we envy the non-Catholic for his alleged liberty.

If before entering this building you looked at the stained glass windows from the outside, what would you have seen? All you would have seen was strips of lead patching odd-sized and more oddly shaped pieces of glass that looked blurred, blackish, and very dirty. You found no design, no figure, no art. And if you had studied those windows a bit closer, it all would have seemed so grotesque, an eyesore, a mess. That was looking at those windows from the outside. Then you came in here and looked at these same windows from within. Everything is changed, magnificent. The designs stand out plainly, all the ugliness gives place to beauty and comeliness and symmetry. It is pretty much the same way with the one who observes the Christian life from the point of view of an outsider. For him, who does not live the supernatural life, who does not penetrate the truth and beauty of that life, the obligations of the Church instead of being a guide to happiness, become an insupportable burden, a lifeless, meaningless obstruction to self-expression. Instead of transforming us, instead of elevating, energizing, divinizing our daily life, Mass and Communion become no more than mere obligations which must be performed and will therefore be gone through as fast as possible.

Not only will our religious life be an empty formula, but even our student life becomes unsatisfactory and meaningless. Why those tedious hours of study, why those boring classroom sessions, why that inner struggle between my sense of duty and that tempting magazine, or that noisy bull session, or that alluring downtown movie? Do you want to know why? Let us be frank in admitting that even here at Notre Dame, even we Catholic students, divorce religion from workaday life. We use prayer, the Mass, and the Sacraments alone with which to worship God when we should be using our periods of study, our tough assignments, our headaches and heartaches, even our morning checks. We are using the Church or the Chapel as our formal place of worship when we should be using the whole wide student world with its fun and its seriousness, its cafeteria and its library, its prefects and its professors. We are using only prayer to get to God when we should be using every effort and every hour. Unconsciously, we are pragmatic materialist and not practical Christians. We are purblind to the supernatural while we are staring and squinting at the natural. We are not piercing appearances, we are not looking inside; hence we fail to find God in our life, nor is our life geared toward God. Not until we love God with our whole heart and our whole soul and our whole strength and our whole mind, i.e. always and everywhere, in the classroom as well as in the dining hall, in our rooms no less than in Church, can we truly say that we have discovered God in our lives, that we are restoring all things in Christ.

But what must we do to reestablish our life in Christ? This seems a very simple procedure, although not necessarily an easy one. One of our own students portrayed it rather forcefully upon a canvas. Against a modern skyline, Christ is seated at table in company with a group of students. He is offering His life and work upon the pattern to God the Father. Two other men, one almost touching Christ's elbow, are bent over the table. They seem broken, dispirited, unable to keep up the fight; they have given up the work, discouraged, yet they are both in the company with Christ, living close to him physically, yet not aware of it. Three other students are also there but they seem to be contemplating themselves, totally unconscious of Christ's presence, almost unconscious of one another. They, too, are not sharing with Christ. A last student is upright and offering his life and his study to Christ's oblation. So many of us are living in the same hall, at least on the same campus with Christ and how many are aware of it to the point of uniting our life to His? That is the secret of making our life supernatural.

By His death on the cross, Our Lord died for us and redeemed us. There was nothing wrong with the sacrifice, it was perfect. By itself, it alone spanned the gulf that separated us from God eternally. While the redemption is perfect, nevertheless, to be applied it needs our collaboration. We must use the bridge that has been put at our disposal. Our free will, our most precious gift from God, must enter into the work. By it we must make an ablation of all our days and unite them to Christ's sacrifice. Gradually we must let Christ influence us, our way of life. He is the "Way" and the way happens to lead to heaven by way of carrying the cross of our daily life, freely accepted and freely united to Christ's big Cross, will make all the difference between heaven and earth; time and eternity.

Let us take a lesson from life. Let us learn from the children of this generation. Let us learn to buy on the installment plan – a home and a fortune in heaven. We can pay for it by daily installments of merits won by the daily offering of our student lives in union with Our Lord's.

In the lives of Cardinal Wolsey and St. Thomas More we have two strikingly similar careers with two entirely different results. Both were prime ministers of Henry VIII of England. Both had served their king well and both were deposed at the whim of their sovereign and deprived of all their honors and possessions. Wolsey, a broken man in health and spirits, declared before his trial, "If I had served my God half as well as I have served my King I would not now tremble to appear before my eternal judge." Thomas More was also disgraced by his king and sent to the executioner's block. When his only daughter tried to persuade him to submit to the king, he asked how many years she could promise him of life. She answered at least twenty. Then he said steadfastly, "And you would have me trade an eternity of happiness for those twenty years of a tortured conscience." Thomas More died a martyr and is today a canonized saint.

Two different students might be leading almost identical lives, at least to all outward appearances. Yet, the final reckoning may reveal a world of difference. The one is living on the gold standard of an earthly goal, the other aims to lay everything on the eternal pattern, on the grace standard of supernatural life. This latter must be our aim. It will be stable and stabilizing. "Seek ye first the Kingdom of God and His justice and all other things shall be added unto you."

Zeal

The subject for this Sunday's instruction is the virtue of zeal. A most fitting topic, you will agree, on the day of Pentecost when in a terrific explosion the divine fire of zeal bolted from the throne of God into the hearts of men. During nine days, a little group of Apostles was persevering with one mind in prayer with Mary, the mother of Jesus, in that great Upper Chamber of the Cenacle. With Our Lord's last command: "Go teach all nations" still ringing in their ears, they awaited the divine Comforter. Now, indeed, He had come; parted tongues, as of fire, appeared and reposed upon the different heads of the little group. Amazement there must have been but also a great peace and joy swelled their breasts. Courage and confidence shone in their eyes. A moment of bewilderment was soon followed by an energetic resolve to tell the world of Christ, of Him who was come to save the world. Aflame with that sacred fire of zeal, they burst open the doors of their voluntary confinement to find, to their utter astonishment, crowds pouring in on their house. Peter spoke and miracle of miracles; they all heard him in their own tongue. Three thousand asked for baptism on that very day.

The Church was founded...its Mission had begun. A worldwide mission, a gigantic mission considering the agents God had chosen; yet from such small beginnings the Catholic Church rose and developed into a numerous family, as the Christian leaven slowly but irresistibly worked its way into the marrow of society, into the masses of the great Roman Empire. Peter and Paul were zealous men, but even they would have accomplished little, had it not been for the help they received from Apollo, from Prisca and Aquilla, and a host of other laymen and women who put their time and their means and their talents into the balance for Christ. Catholic Action is as old as the Church.

By what miracle was the great Roman family of nations changed from a pagan into a Christian commonwealth? Was, perchance, their paganism less selfish than ours? Was the slavery of those days more conductive to Christ's doctrine than the economic slavery of our day? Or rather, shall we not discover the answer in the sincerity with which the early Christians translated the Gospel into their daily life? Those men and women were not only believers; they were doers, actors, and missionaries. They loved God and proved it by serving Him in their neighbor; by bringing Christ to them in their own person. Thus, the slave of the mines converted his fellow-slaves; the toga-ed Roman worked on his friend of the Forum; the craftsman talked to his client of Christ and universal charity and of Redemption that was to make the world a better place to live in. The Roman lady preached her faith to her army of slaves in treating them as brothers and sisters. By the end of the third century all Roman subjects were definitely for or against Christ, not indifferently so, but passionate lovers or rabid persecutors of Christ.

More touching still were the acts of charity of the early Christians, their personal love of their neighbor. "Who among the pagans," asks Tertullian, "would permit his wife to walk through distant streets and to enter the poorest dwellings to visit the brethren? Who would permit them to enter secretly into dungeons for the purpose of kissing the chains of the martyrs? Or to give the kiss of peace to one of the brethren? Or to bring water for the washing of the feet of the saints? Or participate in eating and drinking, to ask for food and even think about it?" This portrayal of the Roman lady's apostolate comes from the pen of an eyewitness; proud Romans though they were and conquerors of the world, they humbly performed their Christian apostolate that so astounded the pagans, to cause them to exclaim in sheer admiration: "See how they love one another."

Charity, real effective, personal charity was the wellspring of the zeal of the early Christians. They loved all men because all are children of the one common Father, who makes the sun shine upon good and bad alike; they loved all men because all men were saved in the Blood of their elder Brother, Jesus Christ. "Whatever you do to the least of these my brethren, you shall have done it unto me." No idle phrase here. With the poor they shared their wealth, with the suffering their sympathy, with the slave and the social outcast, their meals and their interest. "All were of one mind and soul," says St. Luke, "nor was there any needy among them." No selfish clutch on their wealth for the sake of a certain standard of living or social prestige. Like a mighty flood, their charity destroyed class barriers and leveled social distinctions. This Christian love of neighbor was the secret of their success, the wellspring of their zeal.

Charity, we know, is self-diffusive; charity is good, is patient, is not arrogant, is not repulsing. Charity, personal charity, is the master key that will open every heart. Here is a field of apostolate that lies at everybody's door. You need not be a powerful speaker to practice neighborly, Christian love; you need neither wealth nor position. On the Day of Judgment, Christ's sentence will not bear on your assistance at Mass, reception of Holy Communion, your fasts and abstinence, nor will good intentions be of any avail, these are means to an end, but it will call for your concrete acts of love: "I was hungry and you gave me to eat; I was thirsty and you gave me to drink; I was a stranger and you took me in; naked and you covered me; sick and you visited me, I was in prison and you came to me." Why does Christ put such a high value, such heavy stakes upon the Works of Mercy that here He makes them the great test on which we are judged on that final examination? St. John provides the answer: "If any man say, I love God, and hateth his brother, he is a liar. For he that loveth not his brother, whom he seeth, how can he love God whom he seeth not? And this commandment we have from God that he who loveth God, loveth also his brother."

These two great realities: the Fatherhood of God which makes us children of God and the Brotherhood of Christ which makes all men brothers, should fill us with a deep sense of our dignity, but also with a keen insight into our responsibilities. Can we afford to see our fellow student lose his soul or even jeopardize his salvation without ourselves being stirred to the depths of our hearts with the desire to help and to win back the prodigal to our Father's house where, as we know, the Father casts a longing look out toward His last son and may be calling on us to bring him back? Can we remain indifferent when so many even of our immediate relations and friends do not posses the supernatural helps that the sacraments provide to the members of the one true Church, and not burn with a holy zeal until we shall have brought them into the one fold of the true shepherd? Pious raving, some will say; am I to importune my friends and become a bore and a killjoy or perhaps a laughingstock? Strange disciples of Christ these would make who set human considerations before eternal values. Moreover, will true zeal not devise 101 ways of attacking without ever becoming a pest? Prayers, sacrifices, and above all, acts of kindness and charity, all this done perseveringly and tenaciously? Do you think that Christ can refuse you such a conquest that is all to His honor and glory?

Catholic action, dear students, is the modern layman's field of apostolate action for Christ. The Church needs a well organized and well instructed laity to check the inroads of pagan thought and pagan living and make the world safe for Christ and Christian living. Individuals are becoming more and more helpless in face of pagan and worldly influences that are carried on the wings of the air into every home; through the radio, the cinema, the press, the fashion. Under the furious onslaughts of the archenemies of God, the Devil and the World, Communism and Individualism, the profession and the home, those God-given ramparts of faith and morals are rapidly crumbling, like a medieval castle under a nourished canon fire. Hence the necessity in which the Church, guardian of souls, sees herself to organize not only a sharp individual resistance, but an organized counter-offensive under the banner of Catholic Action. Every baptized Christian is, not only by right but by duty, an apostle because that indelible mark in his soul makes him a participant in the priesthood of Christ. He has become an organic member of the Mystical Body of Christ and just as every organ and every member of our human body performs a special and irreplaceable function so every Catholic has an apostolate to perform where no other can take his place. We have come to make the virtue of zeal a monopoly of the priest and an article of luxury for the layman. This tendency is entirely false. Just as in the army every private has a special role to fulfill and cannot be properly replaced by his officers, so every layman must do his share, his God-given share, to promote the good of souls and this concerns not only his own self, but those with whom he is in contact – Catholic or Protestant or Jew who may never get any closer to Christ than through him.

In conclusion, let us ask the Holy Spirit on this Day of Pentecost to grant us a spark of that divine fire that transformed the Chosen Twelve from a timid, fearful fisher-folk into staunch defenders and zealous propagators of God's Kingdom on earth. No dreary, forlorn life that of the apostle, but a life that fully satisfies because it spends itself not for trifles, but for God.

Today the world sets before our eyes a beautiful specimen of zeal, the pure, disinterested self-sacrificing zeal of the Mother. She it is who makes the poorest home a paradise by her winning ways, her delicate manners, her tender concern for every one, her sweet smile, in one word: her love. While thanking God for so great a favor, a Christian Mother, while asking Him to bless and protect her in every way, let us learn a lesson from her, let us acquire the motherly touch in winning souls to Christ.

Feast of Christ the King

The Church is celebrating today the Feast of Christ, the King. This feast is of very recent date; it was celebrated for the first time in 1925. At the very time when Pope Pius XI was inaugurating the feast of Christ's Kingship in Rome, a young Jesuit student was finishing his course of theology in Belgium. A few days later, Miguel Pro became Father Pro and started on his way back to his native country of Mexico where the religious persecution was gaining momentum. President Calles had just decreed the death penalty against the celebration of Mass and the administration of the Sacraments. 137 priests and 50 youthful Catholic lay leaders had already fallen victim to the Bloody Terror. This was the Mexico into which Father Pro threw his youth and vigor and devotion to duty. Two hectic years he spent giving retreats to worker and student groups throughout the federal capital and administering the Sacraments. Although hunted and tracked down by the police, his ready humor and presence of mind saved him in several close calls. On November 17, 1927, however, Father Pro was finally betrayed into the Henchman's power.

An enormous crowd had gathered to witness the trial and execution of Father Pro. On his way from the prison cell to the place of execution, one of the soldiers begged pardon of the priest. "Not only will I pardon you," answered Father Pro, "but I'll pray for you. I want to thank you for the great favor you are doing me today." When Major Torres asked if he had any last wish to make known, the Priest answered very calmly, "Yes, I should like to pray a little." He knelt down, made the sign of the cross deliberately, folded his arms, kissed devoutly the crucifix. Then he rose, brushed aside the blindfold offered him by a soldier, and turning toward the representatives of the Government he said: "God is my witness that I am innocent of the crime imputed to me." With his crucifix, Father Pro traced a huge sign of the Cross over the people adding, "May God have mercy on you all." He stretched out his arms in the form of the Cross, lifted his eyes to heaven and in a reverent but audible voice as if consecrating the host, he pronounced the rallying cry of the Mexican martyrs: "Long live Christ the King." Under a volley of bullets fell a true and loyal subject of Christ the King.

Why is it, dear students, that Pope Pius XI saw fit to establish this feast of Christ the King? What prompted Father Pro to give so generously of his youth and his blood to that cause? To answer these questions is to invite another more fundamental: What should Christ's place be in the life of a man, in our lives? To that question we have God's own answer: "Thou shalt love the Lord thy God with thy whole heart, and with thy whole soul, and with thy whole strength, and with thy whole mind; and thy neighbor as thyself." Translated into daily life this means that the thoughts of our mind, the attachments of our will, the desires of our heart, yes even the movements of our body must be in complete conformity with God's will. The will of God has been made known to us in unmistakable characters in the pages of the Gospel in the life and teaching of our divine Savior, our King. It is the blueprint upon which our lives must be modeled; to be other Christs; to double for Christ is the sublime mission for which we have been selected. This will not mean reproducing Christ's outward actions, his miracles or his journeys or his death on the Cross, but it does mean that we must make Christ's mind and spirit our own. We must carry Him into our work and into our play and into our classroom and into our daily contacts. Christ wants to live His life all over again in each one of us. Once again, He asks to be a young man of 18, sharing everything with us—our hard hours of study, our sleepless nights, our moments of homesickness, as well as our quiet or boisterous hours of fun alone or with friends; he wants to share even the painful embarrassment of a traitorous kiss. Christ has done His level best to be close to us – What are we doing to become nearer to Him? To let Him be the King of our minds, our hearts, and our wills?

For the majority of us it is not a lack of generosity nor one of loyalty that prevents us from giving Christ His proper place in our lives, it is mostly a question of not recognizing Him in our daily life in our daily contacts with our neighbor. It is by coming to the needs of our brother, the student next door or the homesick student or the backward student or the student with a problem to solve, that we fulfill the command of love of neighbor. Paradoxically enough it is when we give Christ to others that we find and possess Him the more: "Whatever you do to the least of my brethren you do it to Me. He who loses his life for my sake and the Gospel's shall find it." It is when Christ seeks out Christ that the bond of the Mystical Body is complete.

Moreover, dear students, none but Christ can ever fully satisfy the craving of the young man for action, for heroism, for idealism. Young men, in the prime of life and energy, have a need for action and self-expression. It is the character and privilege of your age to live your life, to shape your life. It takes youthful energies to play 60 minutes of heads-up football. It is the young men who have always fought the world's battles and are redoing it today. It takes Youth to shape destinies. Christ Himself was no softy, no degenerate, no dreamer or easy chair philosopher. During His public career, He led a very active life, preaching, healing, consoling, and building His future Church. There were days when the besieging crowds would not give Him a moment's respite; to catch a wink of sleep He would have to flee to the mountains or be rowed in a boat over the lake.

He surrounded Himself with young men—fishers—men of action. He had no use for the man who set his hands to the plow and looked back, for the man who wanted Christ to wait till he had bid farewell to his folks or wanted to bury his father. To follow Him, the King, meant instant action, instant and wholehearted service. Christ loved the young. He loved John, the laughter of children. Christ alone will fill your need for action and life. You must let Him control your mind, your heart, your will. Let Him be your leader.

Youth demands and craves for a hectic life; he is by nature a hero-worshipper. This is proved again in the domains of sports and war and achievements. The modern dictators have capitalized on the young man's innate love for glory and adventure. They have demonstrated again how incompetent the human leaders are to satisfy man's thirst for happiness. The leaders of the French Revolution promised complete emancipation for all, based on human equality and brotherly love. Where is love in the modern war-torn world? The Bolshevist promised the material paradise to the down and outer. The paradise will be long coming. The Nazi promised room, elbow room and a place in the sun; the underground shelter may finally be his only place of security.

Christ Himself led the most heroic life – it certainly was not an enviably calm life. Single-handedly he opposed the entire Jewish Aristocracy, unmasking its greed for position and power; He spurned the mob when it wanted to make Him King according to their carnal views, yet He stood up for His Kingship before the Roman Governor when it might have been to his advantage to admit defeat. "Art thou then a King?" asked Pilate. "Thou sayest that I am a King. For this was I born and for this did I come into the world." Christ had set His eyes on Calvary's Hill. Nobody, not even his own relatives and friends, neither His disciples nor His enemies could deter him from pursuing his God-appointed course, from carrying out His God-assigned task. His was a life of true heroism.

Young men need an ideal. They are starving for an ideal to live for, especially in our modern drab way of life, controlled rather by the law of averages and straw polls than by leaders in flesh and blood. In the old-fashioned wars, the leader was seen in the front lines fighting more for his men than with them. Christ is such a leader. He gave every minute of His time, every ounce of His energy, every drop of His blood for His subjects. "Greater love than this no man hath than that he lay down his life for his friend." In Christ we have a leader who hurt no one, but tried to heal all wounds, physical and moral; a leader who to be great shed the blood of no one, but His own; a leader who never tramples anyone under foot, but lifted up all those who came to Him; a leader who conceived no ambitious designs for His own advancement, yet whose name shines above all names; a leader who was humble and meek and self-effaced and today to reach real greatness one must measure up to His standards, follow His teaching, imitate His life. Students, if your ideal is Christ, your success is assured. "Have confidence," He says, "I have overcome the world."

In a church in Copenhagen, Denmark, there is a very remarkable statue of Christ done by the eminent sculptor Thorwaldsen. One day, a tourist came to admire it and was visibly disappointed. He could not find that the reputed statue lived up to its fame. Then someone near him nudged him and said, "Sir, get on your knees and look up into the face of Christ." The visitor complied and immediately perceived the radiating beauty of the work of the artist [which could only truly be appreciated at such an angle].

Let us too, dear students, adopt that attitude of looking up into the face of Christ. Let us study Him in His Gospel, in our neighbor. Distance is invariably a strain on friendship. We must move up close to Him, let Him influence our mind and heart and will. Only a deep personal love of Christ will bring Christ into a war-torn world. The more we discover Him, the more His life and spirit will circulate in us. For we have a king who can give us life, abundant life, never-ending life and happiness provided we let Him control our minds and hearts and wills. For we have a king who holds the solutions to the ills of the world. He needs us, He needs to control our minds and hearts and wills to save the world.

Sermon on Zeal — Final Draft

The subject for this Sunday's instruction is the virtue of zeal. A most fitting topic, you will agree, on the day of Pentecost, on the day on which the divine fire of zeal bolted like a hurricane from the throne of God into the hearts of men. Aflame with that sacred fire and with our Lord's last command, "Go, teach all nations" still sounding in their ears, the small group of Apostles burst open the doors of the Cenacle with an energetic resolve to tell the world of Christ, of Him who was come to save the world.

On that first Pentecost, the Church chalked up an enrollment of three thousand converts; these, in turn, carried their faith with conviction and enthusiasm to the four corners of the earth. From small beginnings the Catholic Church rose and developed into a numerous family as the Christian leaven slowly but irresistibly worked its way into the marrow of society, into the masses of the great Roman Empire. Peter and Paul were zealous men but even they would have accomplished little had it not been for the help they received from Apollo, Prisca and Aquilla and a host of other laymen and women who put their time, and their means, and their talents into the balance for Christ. Thus, within a relatively short time, the great Roman family of nations was changed from a pagan into a Christian community.

The Christians of the early Church might well serve us as models. What was the secret of their fervor, of their success in the Christian apostolate? Undoubtedly, the answer lies in the sincerity with which they translated the Gospel into their daily life. They were not mere believers, but actors, doers, missionaries, missionaries to their immediate neighborhood. Thus, the slave of the mines converted his fellow miners; the toga-ed Roman worked on his friend of the Forum; and the Roman lady treated her army of slaves as brothers and sisters. "Who among the pagans," asks Tertullian, "would permit his wife to walk through distant streets and to enter the poorest dwellings to visit the brethren? Who would permit them to enter secretly into dungeons for the purpose of kissing the chains of the martyrs? Or participate in eating and drinking, to beg for food for the poor?" So many snapshots of the Roman lady's apostolate were taken from her rounds of charity. Proud Romans though they were and masters of the world, they humbly performed their Christian duty that so astounded the pagans, to cause them to remark in sheer admiration, "See how they love one another?!" Do we ordinarily think of the apostolate as something very far removed from us, way out of our reach?

Charity, real effective, personal charity, was the wellspring of the zeal of the early Christians. They loved all men because all are children of the one common Father, who makes the sun shine upon good and bad alike; they loved all men because all were saved in the Blood of their elder Brother, Jesus Christ. "Whatsoever you do to the least of these my brethren, you shall have done it unto me." This is no idle talk. With the poor they shared their wealth, with the suffering their sympathy, with the slave and the social outcast their means and interest. "All were of one mind and soul," says St. Luke, "nor was there any needy among them." No selfish clutch on their wealth for the sake of a certain standard of living or social prestige. Like a mighty flood, their charity destroyed class barriers and leveled social distinctions. Christian love of neighbor was the secret of their apostolate, the wellspring of their zeal. True zeal must begin there. Charity, we know, is self-diffusive; charity is good, is patient, is not arrogant, is not repulsing. Charity, personal charity, is the master key that will open every heart. Here is a field for an apostolate that lies at everybody's door. You need not be a powerful speaker to practice neighborly Christian love; you need not even go out of your way to find an occasion for it; they present themselves to us at every step in form of little services to be rendered. You need neither wealth nor position. On the Day of Final Reckoning Christ's sentence will not bear on your assistance at Mass nor on your fasts and self-imposed penances (these are means to an end) nor will good intentions as such be of any avail, but it will call for your concrete acts of love: "I was hungry and you gave me to eat; I was thirsty and you gave me to drink; naked and you covered me; sick and in prison and you visited me." Why does Christ put such a high value, such heavy stakes, upon the Works of Mercy? St. John provides the answer: "If any man say, I love God, and hateth his brother, he is a liar. For he that loveth not his brother, whom he seeth, how can he love God whom he seeth not?"

These two great realities: the Fatherhood of God and the Brotherhood of Christ, should fill us with a deep sense of our dignity but also with a keen insight into our responsibilities. Can we afford to see our fellow student lose his soul or even jeopardize his salvation without ourselves being stirred to the depths of our hearts with the desire to help and to restore the prodigal to our Father's embrace? Can we remain indifferent when perhaps several of even our immediate relations and friends do not belong to the one fold of the true Shepherd? Pious dreams, some will object: am I to importune my friends and become a bore and a killjoy or be given the cold shoulder? Strange disciple of Christ this one would make who sets human considerations before eternal values! Moreover, will not true zeal devise a hundred and one ways of attacking without becoming a pest? Prayers, sacrifices, and above all, acts of kindness, all this done perseveringly and tenaciously? Christ cannot refuse you such a conquest that is all to His honor.

Catholic Action, and by this we mean organized lay apostolate, is the modern layman's great opportunity for zeal. The need for Catholic lay leadership is great, its possibilities greater still, all of which caused Pope Pius XI to say repeatedly that the world will be saved only through Catholic Action with the layman assuming his responsibilities as a soldier of Christ, a fighting unit of the Church militant. The field for this apostolate is, of course, your immediate environment, those of your acquaintance, the campus and the fellow students. No one is in a better position to know of the students' needs and problems, of his failings and virtues, of his state of mind and of soul than you. You cannot disinterest yourself; Christian charity must make you mourn with him as well as rejoice with him.

The Catholic Action student faces his responsibilities squarely. An instance, a very recent instance, of what a Catholic Action formation can produce in young men: A young lad working in a certain factory is taken to task by his elder fellow workers, bullied and mistreated. He takes the beating manfully. But when he is told to shout, "Long live Lenin!" to please his Communist persecutors, he shouted, "Long live Christ!" to their great surprise. This same young man gave up his job in favor of a Communist who was jobless with a family to support. One would almost believe hearing the acts of the martyrs.

In conclusion, let us ask the Holy Spirit on this Holy Day of Pentecost to put into our souls a spark of that divine fire that transformed the Chosen Twelve from timid, fearful fisher-folk into staunch defenders and zealous propagators of God's kingdom on earth. No dreary, forlorn, empty life like that of the apostle, but a life that fully satisfies because it spends itself not on trifles, but for God.

Today the world sets before our eyes a beautiful specimen of zeal, the pure, limpid, disinterested, self-sacrificing zeal of the Mother. It is she who makes the poorest home a paradise by her winning ways, her delicate manners, her tender concern for every one, her sweet smile, in one word: her love. While thanking God for so great a favor, a Christian Mother, while asking Him to bless and protect her in every way, let us learn a lesson from her, let us acquire the mother's knack of penetrating hearts that we may the better win souls to Christ.

Christmas

On this blessed night, dearly beloved, the holiest night in all the year, we read in St. Luke's simple, sacred Midnight Gospel that a decree went forth from Caesar Augustus that a census of the whole world should be taken. Indeed, it is worthy of note at the very start that the mystery of Our Dear Lord's birth at Bethlehem, so long foretold by the Prophets, should have been accomplished at the command of an earthly monarch, at the scratch of a dictator's pen. Thus it was that Joseph and Mary, as obedient subjects, left the quiet peace of Nazareth and journeyed to Bethlehem, at the Emperor's command; and Augustus, head of the Roman super-state, God that he was by his own appointment, all blown up with human pride and self-sufficiency, was in this matter acting, all-unknowingly to himself, as the instrument of God. And thus it is that the power of God's causality works even today, as it has always worked, quietly, mysteriously, concealing itself, drawing good from evil; so that those who do not believe in God can deny His influence, and those who do believe can scarcely understand.

Augustus decreed the worldwide census so that all, even the least of his subjects, would know that they belonged to Rome; and he sent his officials everywhere to take the census, and to collect that all-important tax, the coin stamped with the Emperor's image. And tonight, dear friends, we are certain that the same edict has gone forth from God, our Emperor, that all of us should be inscribed once more in His Heavenly Kingdom. For in this holy night we realize, as at no other time of the year, that our true citizenship, as St. Paul tells us, is in heaven; and that we are pilgrims and travelers here below, making our way with much hazard and difficulty, toward God, with whom we shall finally be at home. But of all of us our Emperor demands that we pay the tax, the coin stamped with the Image of God.

And so tonight we shall go, as Mary and Joseph went, by way of Bethlehem, and consider once more, with tender love, the message of the Angel to the Shepherds, their hastening to Bethlehem, and the child wrapped in swaddling clothes, and lying in a manger.

It was much the same that night as on any other night on the hills outside Bethlehem. The flocks huddled closely together for protection against the cold and against the wild beasts; the shepherds gossiped sleepily around their fire; and the distant stars blinked coldly through the frosty air, while in the distant city, packed with travelers, men slept, as they always sleep unconscious when God is near. Then, suddenly, unexpectedly, the silent night was radiant and filled with music, and the simple, ignorant peasants fell terrified upon the ground ... until they heard one sweet, clear voice telling them, "Do not be afraid."

"Do not be afraid," dearly beloved, those were the first words spoken by heaven to earth on the night of our Lord's Nativity. And well might those shepherds have been afraid, as they saw the glory of God shining about the Hosts of the heavenly army, and heard the mighty music of the angel's song. They had reason to be afraid. For what, until that blessed night, did they know of God? They knew Him as their Lord Creator, of awful Majesty who had called the vast universe into being out of nothingness, who ruled by a single, easy action of His All-powerful Will the sun and the stars, and the surging of the mighty waters. They knew Him as their Lord Judge, the God of wrath and punishments, and they were right to tremble before His Justice, because they had offended Him by their sins.

But now all this is changed. The angel says, "Do not be afraid, but love; do not be sorry, but rejoice, and be glad. For today is born to you in the city of David a Savior who will save you from your sins." And from that moment, trembling fear was banished as man's first attitude in the face of his God, and tender love took the place of fear. Yes, we fear the Lord of Angels, but we love the little child. We fear the Lord clothed in His awful majesty, but we love Him wrapped in swaddling clothes. We fear Him reigning on the heavenly throne, but we love Him lying in a manger. Dumbly, gratefully, the shepherds looked up and heard the sign by which they were to know him.

"And this shall be a sign to you. You will find an infant wrapped in swaddling clothes, and lying in a manger." And the shepherds hurried off to Bethlehem, and hunted among the rocky hillside caves until they found one all aglow with a heavenly light. And this they entered...And the lovely mother looked up at them, and made them welcome, and graciously gave them permission to look upon the child. Their eyes fell, and there, dear God – there – upon the yellow straw He lay, baby hands upraised, baby hands that made the world, and direct the movements of the stars. Then the shepherds slipped to their knees, beside the faithful Joseph and the patient beasts, and adored the Word made Flesh. Jesus, Mary, Joseph; the adoring shepherds, the timid animals, the manger and the crib – that familiar, lovely picture which has inspired so many masterpieces; but is too beautiful by far to reproduce in any human way:

He came all so still

To His Mother's bower

As dew in Aprille

That falleth on the flower.

But tonight, dear friends, you are the shepherd, hurrying off to Bethlehem, to the new Bethlehem – House of Bread – which is the Church of Christ. And the angels have given you the self-same sign: you will find the infant wrapped in swaddling clothes, and lying in a manger. For our altar is the spotless manger, and soon, at the moment of Consecration He will come alive for us once more, and will be present here under the appearance of bread and wine, the swaddling clothes of the Blessed Sacrament of Holy Eucharist. And there will be given you a privilege denied the shepherds, not even shared in this way by the spotless Mother and her pure spouse St. Joseph: not merely to gaze, to adore, to touch – but to receive the Christ Child into your hearts, to share more richly His Divine Life, to have your Christian lives revitalized under the all-powerful influence of this tiny child who is your Lord and your God. For there can be no greater sign of God's saving love for us than that He, who once was born of the most pure Virgin should daily offer Himself to us to be our food.

Therefore, dearly beloved, with the shepherds we will hasten to Bethlehem, to the manger of the Lord, and with His Mother's sweet permission, we will receive Him into our hearts, ready at this moment to give glory to God in our lives, and to do what in us lies to make peace on earth among men of good will. And one thing more, I ask you in your charity to remember in one Christmas prayer at this Midnight Mass those hundreds of thousands of people who have not yet heard of the great tidings of peace and joy.

Midnight Mass

Gloria in Excelsis Deo.

Glory to God in the Highest and Peace to Men of Good Will! This angelic salute to the newborn King is not only the theme song of Christmas but the refrain of every Sunday Mass and every feast whenever the Gloria is permitted. These simple but symbolic words of the Gloria so clearly express the very reason of Our Lord's coming.

Christ came to restore the world, with all its sin and frustration, to a proper relation with God. All unhappiness of man, stemming from the moment of Adam's rebellion, had to be restored and renewed to serve God's purpose and His glory. Today, then, we are eager to praise God the Father, our Creator, for having sent His only begotten Son. "We praise Thee. We bless Thee. We adore Thee. We glorify Thee!"

For this sublime gift of gifts we hardly know how to thank Him, and in the manner of children we reassure Him over and over again of our loyalty to Him: "We give thee thanks for Thy great glory, O Lord God, Heavenly King, God the Father Almighty!"

And Peace to Men of Good Will! Why this peace? Because the fruits of sin are hatred and disunity – and such has been the lot of all mankind. We have but to run the gamut – our families, communities and nations – and what do we find? Starting with common, everyday quarrels, we see nothing but envy, jealousy, strife, conflict, and even war. Yet the basic desire of all peoples seems to be that for peace, but there really is no peace. Divorces alone cause untold disasters to family peace; unequal distribution of wealth breeds discontent and despair; and beyond these there are the ravages of Communism and other divergence of interests between and among the various nations. Peace, therefore, is a gift of God to man, and Christ was sent to the world with it – as love itself!

This peace, this love, is first of all forgiveness: a deep healing of our wounded nature. Knowing this we sing joyfully in today's Mass: "O Lord Jesus Christ, the Only-begotten Son, O Lord God, Lamb of God, Son of the Father Who taketh away the sins of the world, have mercy on us. Who taketh away the sins of the world, receive our prayer. Who

Images of
Father Putz
& Friends

A Last Blessing

In a eulogy delivered in Moreau Seminary
the evening before Father Putz's funeral,
Father David Burrell reminded listeners of his
old friend and mentor's emphasis on the
priesthood of all the faithful — an emphasis,
Burrell declared, that inspired the pattern
he imposed on seminary education: formation in small groups of young men whose
priesthood would ideally be one of the
galvanizing lay persons "to become Church."

A few days earlier, during a visit from an old
friend, Louis Putz had demonstrated how
fervent and unflagging that belief remained
in the final days of his life. He and his friend,
a layman he had known for many years,
talked for a while and then it was time for the
layman to leave. As the friend rose to go,
the bedridden priest bid him pause.

"Give me your blessing," he asked.

His friend was glad to comply.

✞ You Are Church!